SHARING GROUPS
IN YOUTH MINISTRY

ESSENTIALS FOR CHRISTIAN Youth!

SHARING GROUPS IN YOUTH MINISTRY

WALT MARCUM

ABINGDON PRESS
Nashville

SHARING GROUPS IN YOUTH MINISTRY

Copyright © 1991 by Abingdon Press

This book is printed on recycled, acid-free paper.

Library of Congress Cataloging-in-Publication Data

Marcum, Walt.
    Sharing groups in youth ministry / Walt Marcum
        p. cm. — (Essentials for Christian youth)
    Includes bibliographical references.
    ISBN 0-687-38344-7 (alk. paper)
    1. Church group work with teenagers. I. Title.
    II. Series.
    BV44447.M287 1991
    259'.23—dc20   91-9643
                                        CIP

MANUFACTURED IN THE UNITED STATES OF AMERICA

For Barbara,
my partner in ministry and in life,
who continues to sacrifice much that I might minister to youth.

Acknowledgments

I would like to express my appreciation to those who have made this book possible: to Fred Winslow, for introducing me to this model, and to those who have worked with me as co-leaders in groups. Several of these leaders read this manuscript, and their counsel has been extremely valuable.

I also would like to thank the sharing group members who have enriched my life by sharing theirs. These are the young people from whom I have learned much, to whom I owe much, and for whom I have deep love.

A word of appreciation needs to be given to three people whose support made this book possible: to Gene Roehlkepartain of Group Publishing, for encouraging me to write this manuscript; and to John Gooch of Church School Publications and Paul Franklyn of Abingdon Press, for believing in this project and bringing it to publication.

Contents

Introduction

In the summer of 1982 I was a small-group leader at a high school camp. As I led the group and encouraged the members to openly and honestly share what was going on in their lives, they did exactly that—they began to share their pain, their struggles, and their deepest life issues. I listened to young people talk about things that they never had told anyone. They were saying things that they desperately needed to say but had been unable to say because they never had found a place to share and people to listen. It was one of the most moving experiences of my life. I felt the presence of God in a way that I never had experienced it before. That experience changed the direction of my ministry.

This book was born in that small-group experience. It was born in the realization that teenagers need a place to talk, a place to share the things that they care about most. They need a safe environment and people who will listen. What I discovered was the power of the sharing group model.

When I returned home from camp, the youth from my church wanted to participate in an ongoing group. They did not want to wait a year to experience the kind of love and support they had experienced that week at camp. In the beginning we had many struggles. At camp we had a curriculum; at our church we decided that our lives would be the curriculum. We made a lot of mistakes, but we learned from those mistakes. The group became a standard part of the ministry that our church offers youth. Just as Sunday school, evening fellowship, choir, and Bible study are a regular part of our calendar, so also the sharing group is a regular part of our calendar—to meet needs that the other activities are unable to meet.

This sharing group model has spread to other churches in our area. It has taken on a variety of forms as youth ministers and volunteers have adapted it to meet their needs. After comparing experiences with group leaders in my church and in other churches, I realized that there is a need for a guide that helps group leaders set up and lead sharing groups. This book is an attempt to share what those of us who have led sharing groups have learned, so that sharing groups may become a significant part of youth ministries everywhere. Included are both the mechanics, or "how to's," and the rationale.

This book is for any adult who works with youth, whether he or she be a professional or a volunteer. Anyone who senses the need for this kind of group and who has a vision of the difference that such a group can make in the lives of youth can use the sharing group model in his or her ministry. The purpose of the book is twofold: 1) to provide the conceptual framework and the resources needed to set up and lead sharing groups in the church, or to incorporate elements of the sharing group model into the youth program; and 2) to stimulate thought about the youth group and its needs. To further the second purpose, Reflection Questions to guide the group leader's reflection and Training Tools to help the group leader process this information with a group of adult leaders are provided at the end of each chapter.

This guide will help adults who work with youth to empower their youth to be involved in peer counseling in a group setting. It will serve as a general guide for what is appropriate and feasible in the local church setting. It is not intended, however, to be a complete guide for pastoral care and counseling in the group setting. When ministering to youth in a sharing group, the group leader must be sensitive to the level or degree of a youth's problem and must acknowledge when it is appropriate or necessary to refer a youth to a professional for counseling. How does the group leader know when it is appropriate or necessary? The warning signs will vary according to the situation, but the key is that the untrained group leader—the group

SHARING GROUPS IN YOUTH MINISTRY

leader who is not a professional counselor—must never assume that he or she knows what to do. In other words, the group leader always should seek the advice and counsel of a trained professional when dealing with angry, troubled, or emotionally disturbed youth. Also, because it is impossible to address all possible situations and problems that might arise in the sharing group setting, the group leader is advised to consult the appropriate professionals and resources when confronted by legal or ethical considerations.

Bearing One Another's Burdens

When Rosa was in the second grade, her parents divorced, and she went through a bitter custody battle. Now Rosa is in the ninth grade, and she still is trying to come to terms with some of the things that she experienced. In her sharing group she talks about the anger she feels toward her mother for ending the marriage, and she works on restoring that broken relationship.

Like Rosa, Beth is trying to work through a painful experience from her past. When she was in the fourth grade, her mother was killed. For years Beth held the pain and the anger inside. She was unwilling to talk to anyone about what had happened or what she was feeling. When Beth entered the seventh grade, she became part of a sharing group. For the first time since her mother's death, she began to deal with the tragedy that she had lived through. Five years later, she continues to receive support and love through her sharing group as she struggles with what has happened to her family.

Rick's greatest struggle is with his parents. Rick, a sophomore in high school, wants more freedom than his parents are willing to give him. He and his parents are involved in an ongoing conflict which is painful for everyone. In his sharing group Rick finds support from peers who understand what he's going through. He also gets ideas about how to communicate more effectively with his parents, and sometimes he receives loving confrontation. On more than one occasion the group has helped Rick to see his parents and his relationship with them in a different light.

Dave has been through no great personal tragedies, and he does not have any major conflicts. He comes from a ''healthy'' family, and he has had a happy childhood. In his sharing group Dave is able to give love, support, and strength to the others. Although he has no large-scale problems at the present, he deals honestly with many of his daily struggles.

For Terri, the sharing group is a bridge to the normal world. For several months she has been hospitalized in a drug rehabilitation program. To prepare her for reentry into the normal world, the hospital allows her to participate in a sharing group in a local church. In the group she works on trusting herself and others as well as building self-esteem, healthy relationships, and positive values.

Rebecca, a junior in high school, is a natural leader. She is a sensitive listener, and she has the ability to ask the right question at the right time. For two years she has been the co-leader of her sharing group. When the adult leader cannot be there, Rebecca is responsible for running the group. Church policy requires the presence of an adult, but the substitute sponsor and the group members know that Rebecca is the one who makes the group work.

No one is sure why Bryan is in the sharing group. He is extremely shy, and he never speaks unless someone asks him a direct question. But Bryan never misses a session. He is always the first to arrive and one of the last to leave. One group member has observed that Bryan seems to be happiest when he is in the group session. In the intimate sharing that goes on in the group, Bryan has found something that is missing from the rest of his life.

Although the names have been changed, all of these stories are true. Each of us has youth like these in our church. What is different about these youth is that they have been helped by caring adults and peers in a sharing group. These teens have been helped because their local churches have provided the opportunity for them to deal openly and honestly with important personal issues. In each church are caring adults and peers who have been willing to invest time, to listen, and to care. In a very literal sense, these adults and youth, as well as their churches, are striving to fulfill the apostle Paul's call to "bear one another's burdens" (Gal. 6:2 NRSV).

What Is a Sharing Group?

The kind of group described in the preceding paragraphs is known by many names: sharing group, dialogue group, support group, growth group, prayer and share group, and so forth. Basically, they all are the same. A sharing group is a group in which the members agree to give one another support with problems and struggles by sharing, listening, and following a few simple guidelines.

Three important elements are found in all sharing groups.

1) Sharing groups provide an opportunity to share—a time and a place for teenagers to express their feelings, experiences, and thoughts—to talk about what is important to them.
2) Sharing groups provide people who are willing to listen and to be there for one another—caring adults and peers who are committed to helping one another.
3) Sharing groups provide a safe environment, controlled by simple guidelines, in which sharing can take place. The kind of sharing and support that goes on in a sharing group usually does not happen on its own. A nurturing structure must be in place.

A New Form of Ministry

In many ways the sharing group model is not new. Encounter groups and growth groups became popular in the late sixties and early seventies. Many of the basic ideas began even earlier. By the early seventies, professional psychologists and other counselors who were also Christians began to write books that adapted these principles for the local church setting. In 1972 Howard Clinebell's book *The People Dynamic* was published. In 1977 this book was reissued with the title *Growth Groups,* and it contained a chapter entitled "Youth Growth Groups—Identity Formation." The basic idea of the sharing group and all of the tools used in sharing groups have been around for almost twenty years. What is new is that some churches are offering sharing groups as part of their regular youth ministry programs to provide an intentional opportunity for youth to deal with their struggles and problems. The weekly schedule of some churches now includes sharing groups as well as Sunday school, youth group, choir, and Bible study.

Sharing groups differ from the other forms of ministry offered in youth programs. Unlike Sunday school, Bible study, confirmation classes, and many other forms of ministry, there is no curriculum to be covered. There is no data to be learned; there are only lives to be shared. The youth are the curriculum. Their lives—their joys, sorrows, pains, and struggles—are what a sharing group is all about. Personal depth sharing is not a by-product or something that happens in the process of doing something else. The group exists for the purpose of providing an opportunity to share and to process what is going on in the lives of its members.

Sharing groups also differ from formal counseling or therapy. Trained professionals are not necessary in the typical sharing group. In my church, only one of eight adults who work with sharing groups has had formal training in counseling. Another difference between sharing groups and formal counseling or therapy is their goals.

Therapy Groups Versus Groups that Are Helpful

In *The Mental Health Ministry Of The Local Church,* Howard Clinebell, a pastoral psychologist, makes a distinction between group therapy and groups that are therapeutic, or helpful. According to Clinebell, the two are not the same.

Should the typical church group be thought of as a form of group therapy? Definitely not! Group therapy is one form of psychotherapy. It is an effective instrument only in the hands of a well-trained group therapist. Any general attempt to convert church groups into therapy would produce widespread (and justified) resentment and would miss the broader educational, prophetic, and service goals of a church. Church groups in general cannot and should not be "therapy" groups. . . . [1]

With this warning as a backdrop, Clinebell then argues that we can have groups in our churches that utilize many of the tools of counseling and that these groups can be extremely helpful. He is particularly interested in groups that focus on self-understanding, the ability to deal openly with feelings and problems, and groups that provide the opportunity to grow in health of interpersonal relationships.[2]

Sharing groups are very much in line with Clinebell's guidelines. Sharing groups are not formal therapy groups; however, they are therapeutic. They utilize many of the insights and skills developed within the counseling field to help youth who are basically "normal" but who need love and support.

Clinebell calls these kinds of groups *modified therapy groups.* What he has to say about them is helpful to anyone who is starting a sharing group.

> A modified therapy group retains certain features of group psychotherapy—the goal of growth in self-awareness, the encouragement of honest discussion of those feelings which are "off limits" in most social groups, and the focus on the personal concerns of the members.[3]

There is, however, a real difference between therapy groups and sharing groups: sharing groups do not attempt to bring about "radical personality changes."[4]

Several of the teenagers described in the beginning of this chapter could benefit from formal counseling or therapy. Some of them, like Terri, are involved in therapy and also are in a sharing group. When Terri first entered the sharing group, she was quick to note the difference between the sharing group at church and the therapy group at the hospital. Her therapy group was analytical of everything, was very goal oriented, and was highly confrontational. It also was run by professional therapists. Her sharing group, on the other hand, was more supportive and nurturing. In the sharing group she worked on establishing trust and healthy relationships. Unlike the therapy group, the church group was run by caring adults and peers with little or no formal training in counseling.

Most of us are not certified therapists, but we do not have to be therapists or trained counselors to use some of the tools that modern counseling provides. The difference between a certified therapist and an untrained sharing group leader is a matter of depth and skill level. We can minister to youth at one level; trained professionals can help youth at another level.

What Sharing Groups Offer a Youth Program

Introducing sharing groups into a balanced youth program adds a new dimension to the ministry offered to teenagers. Adolescence always has been a time of intense personal struggle. Today's youth face many additional hardships and pressures. The result is that many of today's youth spend their teen years weathering both developmental and environmental crises. They struggle with who they are and who they will be. They struggle with their parents and with their peers. According to a 1986 study, 20 percent of today's teens suffer from mental disorders. Of those who are considered normal, 20 percent feel emotionally empty and another 20 percent admit to being confused most of the time.[5]

Depression, suicide, chemical abuse, and a host of other problems are examples of the profound effects of stress in the lives of today's teens. Most youth lack the skills to deal with the stresses they face. A University Of Minnesota study conducted in 1987 reported that the top-ranked coping mechanism for dealing with stress among teens was listening to music. Other highly ranked coping methods included making decisions alone, daydreaming, watching television, swearing, crying, and shopping. Sharing and talking through problems were not highly rated. Talking to mom was number thirty-one on the list; dads came in at number forty-eight. Clergy, teachers, and counselors tied for last place.[6]

Today's youth need help. Some of them need help from trained professionals, but most of them simply need the help of caring adults and peers—the kind of help that adults who work with youth are prepared to provide.

When Christi's brother separated from his wife and moved back home, the whole family was thrown into turmoil. Christi was especially upset because her brother had been the center of attention through a long series of crises. Now, as the family struggled with this latest crisis, Christi's needs and concerns were pushed into the background one more time. Christi did not need therapy, but she did need a place to vent her anger and frustration and caring friends who would listen.

In one session of the sharing group, Rick became very agitated and began to rattle off all the things that were bothering him. His outburst culminated with these words: "No one ever really listens to me. All my parents and friends do is give advice! No one cares!" For twenty minutes the twelve people in the room tried to give Rick what he desperately needed: they listened.

Sue became hysterical in one group session. A few months ago her grandmother died suddenly, and no one in the family wanted to talk about it. It was just too painful. When Sue became hysterical, one of her friends reached over and held her. For the next ten minutes Sue sobbed while her friend held her. Afterward, Sue said that what she received from the group was what she had needed for weeks—to be heard, to be held, and to cry.

To be held, to be heard, and to have a place where youth can share their feelings and talk about the things that are really important to them—these are the things that a sharing group can provide. As adults, many of us are acutely aware of our limitations. Most of us are not professional counselors. All of us face time limitations. We need a tool, a handle that will help us to help teenagers. In the sharing group model, twelve to sixteen youth can be helped in a one-and-a-half to two-hour session. Even if each youth is not the focus of the group, all learn and benefit from helping others in the group.

After working with sharing groups for several years, I can see the benefits in the lives of the youth in our church. These are some of the more obvious benefits of the sharing group experience.

Youth Are Helped with Their Struggles

The most obvious benefit of sharing groups is that youth are helped with their struggles. They receive the support and care they need to weather a crisis or to work through important and often painful life issues.

Youth Develop Deep, Caring Relationships

Members of a sharing group become very close. They develop the close koinonia or fellowship that the New Testament speaks of and that many of us long for in our groups. For many youth, this is their first real experience with healthy intimacy.

Youth Develop Problem-Solving Skills

A sharing group is literally a laboratory in life. What is learned in the group is used over and over outside the group. Learning how to heal one broken relationship helps an individual to work on other relationships. Learning how to weather one crisis helps an individual to face the next crisis.

Youth Receive Training in Love

Our youth know that the commandment to "love one another" is at the very heart of our faith; yet, often we have done little to teach them how to love. Some teenagers come from homes in which they are not taught this crucial skill. A sharing group provides training in love. It provides opportunities to fulfill the love commandment.

Youth Have Profound Spiritual Experiences

A somewhat surprising benefit of the sharing group is the depth of spiritual experience that can occur. As a member of a secular therapy group, I was surprised to discover that a part of my group experience was a profound sense of God's presence and grace. The youth in our church report the same sense of God's holiness in the midst of sharing one another's lives.

There is something about opening our lives to one another that puts us in the presence of God. One of the most profound experiences of God that I have had was the first time that Beth shared her feelings about her mother's death. I thought of these words from the story of Moses and the burning bush: "Take off your shoes, for you are standing on holy ground." I and the other members of the group were on holy ground as Beth let us share one of the most intimate moments of her life.

Sharing Groups Are Time Efficient

One benefit of sharing groups is more practical than the others. In a sharing group setting, we can touch the lives of a lot of youth in a relatively short time. It is a matter of stewardship. I have to choose how I spend my time each week. When I'm in the sharing group, I never worry if what I'm doing is a good use of my time. Having contact at that level with that many youth probably is the best thing that I do with my time the entire week.

Sharing Groups Offer a Variety of Formats and Settings

A final benefit of the sharing group model is that it is extremely flexible and adaptable to a wide variety of situations. Groups can be short-term or ongoing. They can be open to any youth, or they can be designed for teenagers with particular needs. Elements of the model and specific skills and tools used in the sharing group setting can be used in other settings such as Sunday school, Bible study, and youth group.

The Short-Term (One-Shot) Model. The short-term or one-shot model was developed in a summer camp for senior highs where it was used in conjunction with a curriculum. Because of its brevity, this model is ideal for camps and retreats. In a short-term or one-shot situation, the sharing group format is used to facilitate sharing and bonding. This design also can be used for group building, for topical events, and for spiritual growth.

A discipleship or spiritual growth group basically functions like a sharing group. The only difference in this kind of group is the addition of a curriculum that focuses the sharing on faith issues and struggles. Groups such as this are mentioned in the chapter "Retreats" in David Stone's *Spiritual Growth In Youth Ministry*.[7]

Another function of the short-term model can be to resolve crises. If there is a problem in our youth group or if the youth have a problem when on a trip, the youth call for a sharing group with whomever is present.

The Ongoing Model. Ongoing groups also can take on a variety of forms. The sharing groups in our church are for anyone who wants to participate. There is no set theme or agenda. Groups in other churches are keyed to special needs and issues, such as divorce, death, life transitions (e.g. graduation), parent/youth communication, and so forth. Some churches have made a sharing group time part of their regular Sunday evening program. In addition to a snack supper, a program, and worship, these groups spend from ten to thirty minutes in Intensive Care Groups, or ICUs.

The possibilities are literally endless. There is a real need among today's youth for what a sharing group can offer. Many youth programs could benefit in a variety of ways from incorporating elements of the sharing group model into their ministries.

* * *

A sharing group can be a valuable tool for helping youth to deal with life's issues. It doesn't take a degree in counseling to help youth. One simply has to be sensitive, caring, and willing to listen. Most of us who work with youth already are doing this in some fashion. A youth calls us at home or approaches us at church. A sensitive issue arises in a Sunday-evening youth program or a teen drops by to talk. In addition to helping us become more intentional in the help we give to youth, a sharing group also can help us to mobilize the resources of peers.

REFLECTION QUESTIONS

1. Review the list of youth in your group. What are the needs of each one?
2. Which needs could be met in a sharing group setting?
3. If you were to start a sharing group, which model would be most appropriate for your setting?

TRAINING TOOLS

1. Begin by carefully reviewing the material in this chapter. What stands out?
2. Does everyone have a clear understanding of what a sharing group is? Arrive at a consensus and write it for all to see.
3. Discuss what a sharing group would offer your youth program that currently is not being offered. How would a sharing group be different from your current youth program?
4. Why do you want to have a sharing group in your church? What are your personal hopes and expectations? How realistic are they? Compare answers.
5. Create a list of potential sharing group participants. Who would benefit? What are their needs? What kind of help could you offer these youth in a sharing group setting?

Biblical and Theological Foundations

At a youth leader training event, one sponsor attending the workshop on sharing groups expressed concern about the use of such groups within the local church. The issue for this adult was not whether or not we had the ability to offer such a group. This adult, who is deeply committed to teenagers and has worked with them for years, put it bluntly: "Since so many of our young people have so little time and are so illiterate on even the basics of the Christian faith, shouldn't we put our efforts into teaching the Bible to our youth and concentrate on teaching them what they need to know to be disciples of Christ?"

This question needs to be addressed. What is the connection between the ministry that a sharing group can offer and the ministry that the local church is called to offer today's youth? What are our biblical and theological foundations for such a ministry?

Why Should We Be Involved in This Kind of Ministry?

Many objections to sharing groups can be raised. On one side are people who are concerned that what happens in a sharing group is counseling. Since most of us are not trained counselors, they conclude that we should not be involved in sharing groups. On the other side are those who are concerned that this kind of ministry sidetracks us from our real ministry.

In reality, however, most youth leaders already are involved in this kind of ministry. We give love, support, and counsel. We listen to our young people's struggles, joys, and pains. We do this every week—in Sunday school classes, in youth group meetings, in Bible studies, on the phone, in the hall, on retreats, and at camps. A normal week is made up of these encounters. We stop to talk with a young person in the hall. He or she suddenly begins to cry and tells us that his or her parents are getting divorced. We get a phone call late at night. A member of the youth group is upset because a friend has been injured or killed in an accident. A youth drops by and wants to talk. One of the youth comes by just to get a hug because it has been a bad day or week. During a program, a young person makes a comment that lets you know he or she is struggling with an important issue.

This kind of support and nurture is not secondary to our ministry. It is at the heart of what it means to be a church; it is at the heart of any valid ministry. Sharing groups extend a caring ministry that Jesus himself modeled.

Biblical Foundations

The model for a caring ministry that takes seriously the concerns of others is Jesus. Jesus identified strongly with the pain of others. He spent his entire ministry getting involved in peoples' lives. In the gospel of Luke, Jesus' ministry begins in his hometown of Nazareth with a powerful identification with the pain and suffering of others. Luke 4:16-21 narrates Jesus' deliberate choice of a passage from the book of Isaiah: "The Spirit of the Lord is upon me, because he has anointed me to bring good news to the poor. He has sent me to proclaim release to the captives and recovery of sight to the blind, to let the oppressed go free, to proclaim the year of the Lord's favor" (Luke 4:18-19 NRSV). Jesus then adds that these words are being fulfilled even as they listen.

Throughout the gospels a consistent portrait of Jesus emerges—a portrait of one who cared, who listened, who got involved, who healed, and who cast out demons. In Matthew 11:2-5, Jesus uses this caring ministry as evidence that he is the Messiah. When John the baptist sends his disciples to ask if Jesus is the Christ or if they are to wait for another, Jesus replies, "Go and tell John what you hear and see: the blind receive their sight, the lame walk, the lepers are cleansed, the deaf hear, the dead are raised, and the poor have good news brought to them" (Matt. 11:4-5 NRSV). This concern for others was not secondary to Jesus; it was at the heart of his ministry. His ministry was not merely a ministry of verbal proclamation; it was a ministry of involvement.

Jesus calls those of us who would be his disciples to be involved in the same kind of ministry. The love commandment is central to the New Testament. In the gospel of John, Jesus makes love the hallmark of the believer when he says, "I give you a new commandment, that you love one another. Just as I have loved you, you also should love one another. By this everyone will know that you are my disciples" (John 13:34-35 NRSV). Much of the historic ministry of the Christian church grows out of this mandate. We cannot love God without loving human beings (I John 4:20). We cannot love those around us without caring and responding to their needs. We cannot love the teenagers whom God has placed into our care without taking seriously their concerns, their joys, their struggles, and their pains. This is why the church historically has been involved in schools, soup kitchens, hospitals, youth groups, and counseling.

As Christians, we are held accountable not only for what we do, but also for what we fail to do. In the description of the last judgment in Matthew 25:31-47, Jesus not only blesses those who fed the hungry, gave drink to the thirsty, welcomed the stranger, clothed the naked, and visited the sick and imprisoned, but he also condemns those who failed to do these things. If we are able to help another, then we should. If we have the tools to help our youth deal with their pain, then we should use them. If we have a way to help teenagers deal with all that is going on in their lives, then we should do everything in our power to provide that opportunity. This is where ministry is born.

Most Christians would affirm this, yet some of us are reluctant when it comes to the ministry of counseling. Remember that one of the mandates we have as a church is to heal others in Jesus' name. In Mark 3:15, Jesus specifically gives his disciples the authority to heal. In James 5:13-16, healing is linked to prayer and touch. Some traditions are tempted to pass over this mandate too lightly. There are those who are uncomfortable with some forms of healing ministry. Others assume that healing has been delegated to the professionals in secular society. Whatever the reason, many of us make little attempt to be actively involved in healing ministry.

Contrary to what many would have us believe, healing is comprehensive and wholistic. Healing can be physical, mental, emotional, spiritual, or relational. Just because there are professionals who can conduct certain forms of healing better than we can does not mean that we should abandon a healing ministry.

This is the ministry where sharing groups fit in—the healing ministry. In sharing groups youth are able to "bear one another's burdens" (Gal. 6:2 NRSV). They are also able to "pray for one another" (James 5:16 NRSV). We can "lay hands" on one another with hugs, listening ears, love, and support. Our young people can continue what Jesus did and what Jesus has asked us to do: to heal the brokenness of others in his name.

Theological Foundations

The ministry offered through sharing groups gives expression to many of the key theological foundations of the church's life. Likewise, these theological concepts shed light on what we are trying to accomplish in the ministry of sharing groups.

Ministry

Clearly, what happens in a sharing group is ministry. What we do in a sharing group is minister to the needs of young people in the name of Jesus Christ. Although some might question the validity of some programs or activities in the local church considered to be "ministry," those of us who have had the privilege of being with young people as they express their pains and struggles would not question the validity of the sharing group experience as ministry in the purest sense—serving others in Christ's name.

Incarnation

Just as the love of God is incarnational, so also must our love be incarnational. Our love for youth means nothing unless it becomes incarnated in what we say and do. Our ministry to young people must be enfleshed in their lives—in their world, their struggles, their problems, and their joys. When we take time to listen to teenagers, we enter into their world. The gospel that we talk about in other settings suddenly becomes real in their lives. God's love can be seen and felt in our love and the love of the group. Our touch and our concern express God's love.

Suzi's life has been shattered by betrayal. For her, the word love has only negative meaning. By taking time to listen to her in the sharing group, I not only minister to her hurt and pain but I also model unconditional love. This helps Suzi to experience the love of God as it is expressed through the love of a believer. This is ministry at the deepest level. God's love becomes incarnate in the love of the group.

Reconciliation

We live in a broken world. Young people are all too familiar with broken relationships. Youth are alienated from their parents and from one another. Some young people are alienated from parts of themselves. Often youth are alienated from God.

In II Corinthians 5:18-19, the apostle Paul says that God "has given us the ministry of reconciliation . . . entrusting the message of reconciliation to us" (NRSV). After years of working in sharing groups, I am convinced that most of what goes on in these groups is reconciliation in one form or another. Most of the time it is reconciliation on the human level—young people bringing together pieces of their broken lives, working on broken relationships with parents and peers. At times, however, reconciliation with God takes place.

Bill is angry with God for the death of a close friend. His anger spills over into his other relationships and begins to affect his whole life. With the help of the group, Bill is able to work through that anger. As he processes his hurt, his confusion, and his anger, he comes to peace with his friend's suicide. He no longer feels the need to blame God or to dump his anger on his friends. Relationships are restored. This is the ministry of reconciliation. The church, in the form of a group of believers in a sharing group, is actively involved in the ministry of reconciliation.

Grace

The most powerful experience of grace that I have ever had was in a group very much like a sharing group. It happened when I realized that the group knew everything about me, even my deepest secrets, but still loved me. That was the day that the grace of God ceased to be only a theological term and became a reality in my life. Likewise, when youth expose their pain, suffering, and guilt—when they allow others to see what they usually let no one see—and discover that they still are loved and accepted, they experience grace.

Many young people are burdened by painful experiences and failures. Some have been abused. Some carry the guilt of mistakes. Some simply feel unloved and unlovable. We often talk about grace in the church, but do we provide places where our young people can actually *experience* grace? The look on a young person's face who has shared a part of himself or herself and has found love and acceptance rather than rejection is something to be treasured.

Faith

Much has been written about the connection between our ability to trust and ultimate trust.[1] Our ability to trust God, to have faith in God, is linked to our ability to trust others.

Many youth have had painful life experiences that have crippled their ability to trust others. How can we ask these youth to trust God when they don't know what trust is? If we help them to learn to trust, we also help them to grow in their ability to trust God. The sharing group model and guidelines presented in this book are designed to facilitate trust. A teenager who has lost the ability to trust others because of painful experiences can relearn how to trust others through the relationships that are fostered in a sharing group environment.

Rennie's ability to trust has been destroyed. On two occasions, members of her family sexually abused her. Both incidents took place when she was a young child, but the effects are still evident. At the deepest level of her being, Rennie does not trust others. She knows that if she trusts others, they will take advantage of that trust. Our group has worked with Rennie for over two years. We can't change what happened in the past, but we can be trustworthy in our relationships with Rennie. We can show her that not everyone will betray her trust. Rennie is slowly learning to trust the group members. She has a long way to go, but she is beginning to trust others for the first time in ten years.

A Contemporary Extension of the Ministry of Jesus

As has been illustrated, the ministry of sharing groups is very much in the historic tradition of the church. Ministry meets a need, whether it be restoring a broken relationship with God, feeding a hungry person, or providing a place where youth can deal with the things that are important to them.

Some of what we do in sharing groups may appear to be the same as what those outside the church do. The difference is not our methods but our motivation. Modern group dynamics may give us tools to work with, but our motivation is theological rather than analytical or psychological. We respond to the love that we have experienced through Jesus Christ by loving those whom God has entrusted to our care. We follow Christ's injunction to feed my sheep, to bear one another's burdens, to pray for one another, and to heal that which is broken—and we do it in Jesus' name. By doing this, we continue the ministry that Jesus began and then entrusted to those who would be his disciples.

A Community of Care

It is neither accidental nor incidental that Jesus called his disciples into a relationship with himself as well as a relationship with one another. Community is at the heart of the Christian faith. Through our relationships with one another, we learn what it means to have a personal relationship with God through Jesus Christ. By developing trust within a community, we learn what it means to place ultimate trust in God.

Through the ages the Christian community primarily has expressed its life in corporate ways. The community nurtures and supports the individual believer. It also confronts and holds the believer accountable for his or her behavior. The sharing group embodies both of these elements—nurture and accountability. Through the sharing group experience, youth learn what it means to be in community with other believers. They learn how a group can support them and how they can support others. They also learn that the community can be a source of confrontation and accountability. Members of a sharing group "bear one another's burdens" in both ways. Although the sharing group uses tools of contemporary counseling such as listening skills, the sharing group goes beyond listening in a non-judgmental way. It operates within a distinct value system and presupposes a community that extends beyond the group itself.

The locus for most sharing groups will be the local church. The youth who are in the group will be the same young people who worship together and share the life of the congregation. All of this is value laden. It gives the group permission to work with the individual in additional ways. Values clarification has a place in the sharing group setting, as does decision making. In this sense, the sharing group has elements in common with covenant or discipleship groups. Theories of counseling and particular techniques may come and go, but the basic Christian commitment to the members of the community—to their health and growth—is constant.

REFLECTION QUESTIONS

1. Which scriptures shape your understanding of what it means to be a church?
2. What is your understanding of ministry?
3. In what kinds of healing ministry is your church currently involved?
4. In what kinds of healing ministry should your local church be involved?
5. How does the sharing group model fit in with your understanding of the church, ministry, and healing?

TRAINING TOOLS

1. Lead your group in a Bible study of the following scriptures:

   Luke 4:16-41   Matthew 11:2-6
   Matthew 25:31-46   James 5:13-16
   Matthew 10:1, 7-8   John 13:33-34
   Galatians 6:2   II Corinthians 5:18-19

   What do you glean from these scriptures in terms of the ministry you should be offering the young people of your church?

2. Have the group write definitions of the following terms: ministry, grace, incarnation, faith, reconciliation, agape love. How should these things shape the ministry that you offer the young people of your church?
3. Write a theological statement to reflect 1) your understanding of what it means to be a church in ministry to youth and 2) how a sharing group can fit into this understanding.

3

Putting Your Group Together

Bert was excited about starting a sharing group in his church. He made announcements for several weeks. The young people seemed to be interested. Two teenagers showed up the first night. They seemed to be embarrassed. No one showed up the second week.

Glenda had a lot of interest in her sharing group. She opened the group to anyone who wanted to come. The first night there were a dozen young people. Seven sponsors showed up, including two parents of youth in the group. No one was willing to share.

The first session that Karen held with her sharing group was an incredible experience for everyone. The young people expected to give of themselves and to get a lot out of the group. Andy shared a very personal struggle, and the group jelled. Two years later, Karen's group is still going strong.

What happens before your first session is important. The preparation that you do for your group largely will determine the nature of the group and whether or not the group will get off the ground. Careful preparation will pay off in your first meeting. There are several things to consider as you put your group together.

1. Decide What Kind of Group You Will Have

There are many kinds of possible groups: ongoing groups or one-shot retreats; groups open to anyone or groups keyed to specific concerns; junior high groups, senior high groups, or combined groups; groups that are for sharing only or groups that involve elements of spiritual growth and discipleship. The following chart shows some of the possibilities for groups that utilize a sharing group format.

> **ONGOING GROUPS**
>
> - Sharing groups open to anyone
> - Groups limited to a particular age group:
>   —junior high groups
>   —senior high groups
>   —groups for graduating seniors
> - Groups keyed to specific concerns:
>   —grief recovery groups
>   —leadership development groups
> - Discipleship groups:
>   —covenant groups (such as Branch Groups)
>   —spiritual growth groups which focus on members' relationships with God
>
> **ONE-SHOT GROUPS**
>
> - Small groups at camp that use sharing group guidelines along with a curriculum
> - Small groups on a retreat to debrief experiences
> - Small groups on a trip to wrap up the day
> - One-time groups to deal with a particular issue

This book is written primarily for a typical ongoing sharing group that meets weekly to deal with personal concerns and problems. However, the model can be adapted to fit your setting and needs. You must determine which type of group is right for your church and your youth.

The first decision to make is who will decide what kind of group you will have. Will it be you or the youth? Will parents be consulted? What about church boards and committees? In the churches in our area, the decision usually is made by one adult who is willing to make the commitment to form and run the group. The young people, the parents, and the appropriate church committees or boards are consulted, but the final decision usually is based on whether or not there is a person willing to do the work.

Once you have determined who will make the decision, decide what type of group to offer. Specifically, decide whether the group will be ongoing or short-term and what needs the group will target. You may want to use a survey of youths' needs, such as the one found in Appendix A, to help you make these decisions. You can adapt this survey to obtain the needed information or you can create your own instrument. I suggest conducting the survey in person or on the phone rather than handing out forms. You will be asking for personal information, so you will need personal contact.

2. Choose a Co-leader

Our group had been meeting for six months when we had our first crisis. The group had become close, and the youth were dealing with very important issues. One girl was struggling with how to relate to her gay father, two young people were members of families going through divorce, and two youth were dealing with deaths in the family. The youth had come to depend on the group. It was an important part of their support. The crisis came when I left for a two-week vacation. I had not taken the time to recruit an adult co-leader, and this meant that it would be three weeks before the group could meet. For several of the young people this was a painful and unnecessary crisis. It was unnecessary because I should have taken the time to recruit a co-leader.

Because the teenagers depend on the group, it should meet on a regular basis. However, the reality is that there will be times when the adult group leader cannot be there. Having a co-leader guarantees that at least one adult always will be there so that the group can continue to meet. Having a co-leader also makes it possible to expand the number of groups that can be offered at a later date. If two adults work with a sharing group for a period of time, then both are likely to become skilled group leaders. Later, each adult could lead his or her own group and train new co-leaders.

Be selective when recruiting a co-leader. If there is a trained counselor in your congregation who would be willing to give his or her time, try to recruit this person. It would be wonderful to have the skills and resources of a trained counselor in the group. Unfortunately, this is a luxury that most of us do not have. Recruiting a co-leader usually means recruiting an adult who has had little or no formal training. When recruiting co-leaders, look for adults who possess the following qualities or characteristics.

Adults Who Love Young People

I would rather have a co-leader who loves youth but who has no formal training in counseling than a co-leader who cannot relate to young people but who is a trained professional. The skills that will be used in a sharing group can be taught; genuine care for teenagers cannot be taught.

Adults Who Are Loved by Young People

A certain amount of chemistry is involved in working with youth. Adolescents like some adults more than others. Young people simply are more comfortable around some adults. These are the adults who give the group a warmer environment just by being there.

Adults Who Are Good Listeners

Some adults want to tell youth what to do. These adults are parental. Other adults are natural listeners. Because listening is the most basic and most important skill used in a sharing group, it makes sense to choose adults who have the natural ability to listen.

Adults Who Can Commit

The adult leaders of the group need to have regular attendance. An adult who comes and goes and who cannot make a commitment to be there week after week can be just as disruptive as a teen who does the same thing. Trust begins with regular attendance.

Adults Who Love God

When choosing co-leaders, I do not look for saints, but I do look for adults who have made a commitment to God and who are growing in faith. I want adults who are there to love youth because of their own love for God.

* * *

Rarely is it helpful to make a general invitation for co-leaders, because someone who does not work well with young people might volunteer. It is best to decide whom you want to work with based on your relationship with the individual and the ways that the youth relate to the individual. Then approach this person and try to sell him or her on the idea. You want the best possible co-leader for the group; the young people deserve no less.

Allowing the young people to give input during the co-leader selection process is important. It is wise not to ask the youth for names, because they might get excited about an adult who lacks one or more of the aforementioned qualities. A better idea is to list possible co-leaders and then to ask the young people for their reactions. Another possibility is to ask several youth to help draft a list of possible co-leaders to pass by the entire group. Many churches have youth representatives on boards and committees, including committees that evaluate and hire church staff. Any young person who is mature enough to sit on one of these committees is mature enough to help select a co-leader. These youth must understand the need for confidentiality and must be able to discuss candidly what would make an individual a good co-leader. There is no reason that these youth should not be involved in the process from the beginning. Their reactions may be the determining factor in your decision.

3. Sell the Idea

Bert's group "died" after one session because he did not sell the idea to the group. If you are to make a sharing group part of your church's ministry, then you must sell the idea to three groups: the youth, their parents, and the congregation.

The Youth

The youth are busy. They have little free time. Most likely, you will have to convince them to give up something they already are doing to make time for the sharing group—as well as to convince them that the group will be worth their efforts. The best way to do this is to let the youth experience what happens in a sharing group. Simply telling the youth about the sharing group experience does not do the job. There are a variety of ways to provide an initial sharing group experience for your group.

● *Visit an existing group.* If there is a sharing group in your area, ask if you and a few young people can visit the group. Our sharing group has visitors from other churches every few months. The youth consider this to be a compliment.
● *Form a sharing group on a retreat.* The young people in our church love retreats. Planning a retreat around small-group sharing allows youth to have an intensive experience of the sharing group model.
● *Turn the youth fellowship program into a sharing group for one evening.* There is no reason not to use the evening fellowship time to hold a one-shot sharing group experience. You may want to expand the regular schedule to allow enough time for the sharing group. Sharing and building trust through an experience such as this would make an excellent program.

The Parents

Parents have the right to know what's going on with their children. If parents know what a sharing group can be, then they are more likely to be supportive. Parents in our church often go out of their way to tell me what a difference the sharing group has made in their children's lives. Several parents have allowed their children to attend sharing group meetings even when they have been grounded from all other extracurricular activities. These parents recognize the importance of the group.

It's not what parents know but what parents don't know that can hurt us. After we started sharing groups in our church, we asked one of the youth to report what we were doing to the board. She summarized what we did in the sharing group by saying, "Well, we sit around and gripe about our parents." Several parents and several adults who worked with the sharing groups laughed. They laughed because they knew that it wasn't true. They had the information they needed to realize that the statement about griping said more about that young person than it did about the group.

Because sharing groups are confidential, parents will not be able to ask their children, "What did you do tonight?" However, we can help parents to understand what a sharing group is and does by talking to them in advance. I usually go over the sharing group guidelines with the parents just as I do with the teenagers. This accomplishes two things: it lets the parents know what a sharing group can offer their teenagers, and it assures them that we are not "griping" behind their backs. Parents want what is best for their children. The more information we give them, the more supportive they will be.[1]

The Congregation

The congregation also has the right to know what's going on with the youth. Boards and councils who represent the church and who are responsible for church policy need to be aware of the purpose of the sharing group and the guidelines by which it operates.

If the church trusts the person in charge of the youth ministry, then they generally will trust this person's proposals. Politically, however, it is important to explain what you will be doing to a few "key people," especially if you anticipate some resistance to the idea. Key people would include the pastor, the lay leadership of the church, and respected members of the congregation. It is helpful to present the idea to those who may have objections, thereby defusing possible resistance, and to those who are likely to support the idea and to advocate it to others.

When I was pastor of a church that was starting its first sharing group, I knew that we would have trouble when presenting the idea to the church board. One very vocal board member was opposed to anything new. If you tried to approach him individually, it made him even more suspicious. I also knew that another board member, Mr. Abbott, was the most respected member of the congregation. If he supported something, then the church supported it as well. So I explained to Mr. Abbott in advance what we were trying to do. He loved teenagers, and he thought it was a wonderful idea.

When I made the proposal at the board meeting, the one negative member said, as I had predicted, that he didn't think it was the church's business to do this kind of thing. Several heads nodded in agreement. I began to worry, but Mr. Abbott stood and said, "I like the idea." Sharing groups were in!

The same principle that works with parents also works with the congregation: the more information that you can give them, the better off you will be. An informed congregation is one that will work with you. When a youth explains that "we're griping about our parents," the congregation will be able to laugh because they will know better.

4. Decide Who Will Be in the Group

The makeup of the group is important. Having a balance of different kinds of youth ensures that the group has the right chemistry. When I form a new group, I recruit three kinds of youth.

Young People Who Need the Group

All of us know youth who are hurting, who are struggling with various crises in their lives. I know that Dave is still struggling with his father's death. I know that Greg is torn up because of his parents' recent

SHARING GROUPS IN YOUTH MINISTRY

separation. I know that Sally is shy, lonely, and depressed. These are the young people who stand to gain most from being in a sharing group. They need a place to talk and people who will listen. Ideally, approximately one-third of the group should be made up of these kinds of teens.

Young People Who Have Something to Offer the Group

We also know youth who are natural helpers, who know how to reach out to others. Shelly is "solid." She cares. She is a gifted listener. Dave makes everyone feel loved. Gary is sensitive to others' needs and always seems to know the right thing to say. The young people who are struggling need these youth in the group. They make the group a loving, caring place. Ideally, approximately one-third of the group should be made up of these young people.

Young People Who Want to Be in the Group

After I recruit the first two groups, I issue a general invitation to the group at large. I'm always surprised by who responds to these invitations. There are youth who have serious problems of which I was unaware. There are youth who are "undiscovered" gifted helpers. There are young people who simply want to belong. And there are youth who are just there, although I'm not sure why.

* * *

A sharing group that has a balanced mixture of these three groups works well. Each group needs the others. The sharing group needs young people who are helpers and young people who are in need of what a sharing group can offer. Together they make the group work.

Should you exclude anyone? Personally, I am opposed to excluding anyone as a matter of principle. However, circumstances should be considered on a case-by-case basis. If you know of someone who has a record of breaking confidentiality, then you must decide how to handle the possibility of his or her participation in the group. If two young people from the same family or two teenagers who do not get along with each other want to be in the group, then you are faced with a special problem. None of these things automatically should exclude a person from the group; however, the circumstances should be carefully considered. Although no one solution can solve all problems, offering more than one group can solve several of these dilemmas.

5. Limit the Size of the Group

I usually recruit fourteen to sixteen young people for one sharing group, knowing that some will drop out. On any given week, one or two youth are likely to be absent. Twelve is the *ideal* group size, but eight to ten on a regular basis is a desirable group size.

If the group is smaller than eight, special problems arise. A group with five or six present can work, but they may not have much to say. Groups smaller than five to six tend to die. They just do not have enough people to make them work. On the other hand, groups larger than fourteen to sixteen are too big. Side conversations develop, and all the youth are not focused on what's happening in the group. In large groups there is too much personal agenda and too little time. More young people want to share than there is time for, and group members do not get the attention they need.

6. Set a Regular Meeting Place and Time

Your group never should have to guess whether or not the group is going to meet or where it will be meeting. The group needs a regular meeting time and place. Members will come to depend on the group; it will become an important part of their support structure.

Karen speaks for many of our group members. Her home situation is extremely painful, and she does not feel accepted at school. Each week she looks forward to the sharing group. In the group she finds love, support, a place where she can be herself, and the strength to face another week in a hostile environment. Karen shared with the group that she credits them with literally saving her life on three occasions during the last two years. The pressures and problems were so bad that she almost went under. It was her sharing group that kept her going. Karen didn't need a sporadic, hit-or-miss group. She needed to know that every Wednesday at 8:00 P.M. in the youth lounge her group would be there for her.

7. Choose a Private Place Where You Will Not Be Distracted

When our group began five years ago, we started in the church parlor. It seemed to be the perfect place. It had carpet, soft couches, and chairs. As it turned out, using the parlor was a bad idea. One week a member was working through the suicide of a friend. He was very upset, and talking about his feelings was extremely difficult for him. Right in the middle of his sharing time, a group of adults walked in to investigate the parlor for a wedding shower to be held later that week. On another occasion, a new member of the youth group invited himself into the sharing group when someone was sharing something private and sensitive. It got to the point that we would have two or three interruptions during a typical session. The parlor is the last place to hold a sharing group in our church!

Distractions are harmful to the sharing experience. Even after a brief distraction, it can take a long time to return to the same level of sharing. This is why it is important to choose a quiet place that is out of the way. The sharing group that I lead meets in my home. I disconnect the phone to guarantee us two hours of uninterrupted privacy. Some young people in your group may volunteer their homes. If so, you will have to deal with the presence of parents. Will you really have privacy? Will anyone walk through the room? Will the youth who lives in the house feel free to share? You also may have to deal with parental concerns about meeting in a home.

8. Choose a Comfortable Place

The atmosphere of the meeting room also makes a difference. Our church parlor was wonderful. The sharing group members loved it. It was comfortable. They could take off their shoes and curl up on the sofa or in a plush chair. Others could sit on the carpet. The whole room said "make yourself at home." We also could pull the furniture together to make a "conversation pit" where we could be close.

When we left the parlor because of lack of privacy, we went to a room that was less hospitable. The furniture wasn't right; it didn't encourage the young people to sit together. The young people spread out, and consequently our sharing lost something. Now we meet in a home where we have carpet, sofas, and plush chairs—and we can sit close together. As a result, the depth of the sharing has increased.

The atmosphere of the room can make a difference. It can work for or against you. Look for a room that is warm and comfortable—one that will make your group at ease. Also look for a room where you can arrange the furniture into a "conversation pit." When the youth sit close together, they share more. When they spread out, sharing decreases.

REFLECTION QUESTIONS

1. Who in your youth program would benefit from a sharing group? Of what specific needs and problems are you aware?
2. Whom would you like to be the co-leader? What qualities does this person possess that would make him or her a good co-leader?
3. How will you sell the idea of a sharing group to your youth, to their parents, and to your congregation?
4. Who are the natural helpers that you would like to have in your group?
5. Will you exclude anyone from the group? If so, why? How will you handle the situation?
6. When and where will the group meet? Will the group have the comfort and privacy that it needs?

TRAINING TOOLS

1. Have the leadership team draft a list of young people who could be in the group. Who are the young people with special needs? What are those needs? Who are the natural helpers in your youth group?
2. Plan a strategy for presenting the sharing group proposal to the youth. Do the same for parents and the congregation. Brainstorm possible problems in selling the idea and how you would handle them.

4

Your First Session

You have carefully selected the members of your group. You have a co-leader, a time and place to meet, and a comfortable setting where you will not be interrupted. Your group is present and ready. Now what do you do? How do you guarantee that your first meeting goes well?

1. Prepare the Group in Advance

Before the group members arrive for the first session, make sure that they clearly understand why they are there. They are there to talk about their concerns, struggles, problems, issues, and feelings. They are there to share their lives and to listen as others do the same.

It is dangerous to assume that the young people understand the purpose of the sharing group. Even one young person who misunderstands the group's purpose can undermine the session. Be sure to review the group's purpose with each member prior to the first session. If you take the time to do this, then you will guarantee that all of those who show up at the first session are there for the same reason.

2. Go Over the Guidelines

After you have welcomed the group and have made any necessary introductions, take a few minutes to go over the guidelines in Appendix B. Make sure that every member has a copy. Read and discuss each guideline. Be sure that each youth understands why each guideline is important. As the members do this, they will be telling one another their expectations for the group and for one another.

Ask the youth if they have problems with any of the guidelines. Also ask if they would add other guidelines. Because it is their group, they need to have ownership of the ground rules. Then challenge the group. Let them know that it is their willingness to share that will make the group work and that they will get as much out of the group as they put into it.

3. Open with a Circle Prayer

Begin the session by having the group hold hands or link arms in a tight circle. Invite the members to participate in a circle prayer in which each person lifts his or her hopes and fears to God. You may want each person to finish his or her part by completing the sentence, "Lord, I'm here because . . . ," or the sentence, "Lord, I ask your help to. . . . " Listen carefully as the prayer goes around the circle, and then close the prayer yourself. Try to draw together all that was said and to lift it to God.

4. Share "Highs and Lows"

Take plenty of time to go around the circle and let each person share the "highs and lows" of that week. A high is something good that has happened during the past week: beginning a new relationship, passing a class, getting a driver's license, finding a date for the prom, or whatever the person feels good about. A low is something bad that has happened during the past week: fighting with parents, ending a relationship, becoming sick, failing a class, or whatever the person feels bad about. Encourage each youth to share at least one high and one low. If a person can't think of one, come back to him or her later. If some members have more than one high or low, encourage them to share until they have expressed all their joys and concerns.

This exercise is important because it begins the process of sharing with a very low threat level. It breaks the ice and begins the sharing without making the members nervous. If everyone in the group does the exercise, then everyone is involved in the group process from the beginning. The members share a little of themselves with the group even before the actual sharing time begins.

5. Do the "If I Were to Share" Exercise

Beginning with yourself, have each person speak briefly on the topic of "if I were to share." Tell the group that they have no obligation to respond in any way to each person. Each person is to talk briefly about the most painful thing in his or her life or about a topic that he or she would like to discuss. Role model openness and honesty in your own sharing. If you are candid about your own feelings and share something that involves some risk, then others are likely to do the same.

Listen carefully as the group shares. Be prepared to ask individuals if they would be willing to share more about the issues they mentioned in this exercise. Do not force youth to share; rather, invite them. Often youth are unwilling to bring up a topic themselves, but they are willing and relieved when given an invitation.

6. Decide Who Will Share During the Session

To decide who will share during the session, I usually ask, "Who would like to have some time tonight?" Because there may be some initial awkwardness, it is all right to allow a period of silence. After thirty to forty-five seconds, someone usually will raise his or her hand or will speak. Once this happens, others who want time are likely to speak.

It is helpful, especially during the first few sessions, to talk with some of the members about claiming sharing time before the group session. Some young people are reluctant to speak up but are willing to share if asked. It is good to have three teens who, for the sake of the group, are willing to break the ice by going first. Then, if no one in the group is willing to speak, you can turn to one of these youth and say, "John, you and I talked this week about you taking some time tonight. What's going on?" If you have done this, then you have guaranteed that some sharing will take place in the first session.

When you know who wants some sharing time or who is willing to share, prioritize the sharing order. First priority goes to someone who is emotionally upset or someone who is having a crisis. Second priority goes to someone who is not having a crisis but who has not shared in a while. Last priority goes to someone who is not having a crisis and who has shared in the group recently. This guarantees that those who need help most get it and that everyone in the group has a turn.

7. Begin with the First Person

Once you have determined who will share first, say something such as, "Tell us what's going on." As the person begins to share, use the eight growth factors discussed in chapter 5—especially the skill of active listening. Use the twelve tools for sharing groups discussed in chapter 7 to encourage the individual to continue sharing.

8. Provide Closure After Each Person Shares

When you sense that a person has finished sharing, ask if he or she is ready to stop for now. I usually say something such as, "Is it OK for us to move on to someone else, or would you like more time?" If the person says that it is all right to move on, thank him or her for trusting the group and for sharing. When appropriate, you may want to suggest that the individual hug some or all of the members, especially those with whom he or she interacted. If the individual shared sensitive information or feelings, you may want to ask if he or she is worried about how the group feels about what was shared. If the individual says yes, then invite the group to respond.

Now ask the group how they are doing. Members may have reacted differently to something that was shared. Be sensitive to members who may have become emotional. Encourage the group to share what they are feeling.

9. Move on to the Next Person and Repeat the Process

When you are convinced that the first person is ready to move on and that the group has closure on what was said, move on to the next person and repeat the process. Do not worry if there is not time for everyone, or if you have time for only one person. The entire group benefits from one person's sharing, especially if they are dealing with something significant. It is better to deal in depth with one person and to have the entire group involved in that process than to prematurely move on to someone else because of time pressure. It also is all right for many members to share briefly. Each group and each session is different. The goal for the first session is to show the members that the group is a safe, caring environment in which they can share the things that are really important in their lives. If the session ends with the members wanting to come to the next session, knowing that the group is available to them, then you have accomplished a lot.

10. Provide Closure for the Session

When you are almost out of time and you have had closure with the last person who shared, take a few minutes to provide closure for the entire session. Ask the group members how they feel about being a part of the group. Encourage members to share what they are feeling as the session comes to a close. If you have time, go around the circle and have each person share briefly.

Encourage those who did not share to do so the following week. If some wanted to share but did not get to do so this time, assure them that they will be the first to share at the next session, unless someone is having a crisis.

11. Close with Prayer

Have the group form a circle as they did at the beginning of the session. Close with a circle prayer in which each person completes the sentence, "God, I thank you that. . . . " Follow the prayer with a group hug and individual hugs.

REFLECTION QUESTIONS

1. What do you think will happen in your first session? What are your hopes and fears?
2. Who is likely to share in the first session? How will you handle the situation?
3. Think of three group members who might be willing to break the ice by going first. Who are they? What concerns are you aware of that they could share?
4. What problems might arise in your first session? How would you handle them?

TRAINING TOOLS

1. Have the team brainstorm problems that could arise in the first session. Have the group choose three or four of these and role play how they would handle each situation.
2. If your leadership team is large enough, form a sharing group and experience what you will be asking the young people to do—to share and support one another. The issues to discuss could be how each person feels about going into the first session.
3. Practice having closure in other settings: Sunday school, evening fellowship, Bible study, and so forth.

FIRST SESSION OUTLINE

Task	Tools	Time Required*
prepare group in advance	group purpose statement, Appendix B	several minutes with each youth before first session
welcome group/make introductions		2-3 minutes
review sharing group guidelines	Appendix B	5-10 minutes
open with circle prayer		2-3 minutes
share highs and lows		10-15 minutes
"if I were to share" exercise		5-10 minutes
decide who will share		can be done during the highs and lows and the "if I were to share" exercise and/or before the session
begin with first person	8 growth factors and 12 tools for sharing	as much time as needed (will vary)
provide closure after sharing		2-5 minues
move on to next person and repeat process		as much time as needed (will vary)
provide closure for session		5-10 minutes
close with prayer		2-3 minutes

*Times shown are suggested times. Please adjust time allotments to meet the needs of your group. A first session generally lasts from 1-2 hours.

Eight Factors
in Personal Growth

Have you ever wondered why some well-trained professional counselors, psychologists, and psychiatrists are unable to help others with their problems while other counselors, psychologists, and psychiatrists offer effective help? Or have you ever wondered why some people with little or no training seem to have a natural gift for helping others? Several years ago, a landmark study sought to determine what enables a person to help another. The results of this study conducted by Robert Carkhuff were published in the book *Helping and Human Relations: A Primer for Lay and Professional Helpers.* The book has had a profound affect on the helping community, and many contemporary treatment programs are based on Carkhuff's work. Carkhuff discovered that it is not primarily a formal education in theory that enables one person to help another. Rather, what makes a difference in helping relationships is the presence of eight *growth factors.*[1] Carkhuff isolated and identified eight growth factors that, when present in a helping relationship, help a person to get better. When these growth factors are missing, the person either will not be helped or will get worse. This is true for both professional helpers and untrained volunteers.

The eight growth factors that Carkhuff identified were *empathy* (or active listening), *respect, warmth, concreteness, genuineness, self-disclosure, confrontation,* and *immediacy.* If we want to help youth deal with their struggles and problems, then we must seek to embody these skills and qualities. These qualities are absolutely essential to create an environment in which youth are free to explore significant issues.

Using these growth factors does not require a degree in counseling. Many of us already use these growth factors, to some degree, without being aware of it. All of the growth factors are things that we can develop through practice. This means that those of us who are lay helpers—that is, untrained counselors—can be very effective helpers in many situations. We simply need to know what works—*what* to do in our relationships with young people and *how* to do it. This does not make us professional counselors, nor does it qualify us to do all the things that professionals can do. The growth factors merely help us to be more effective in our helping relationships with youth.

The sharing group model presented in this book is based on the growth factors identified by the Carkhuff study. A sharing group attempts to create an environment in which these factors are present.

1. Active Listening

A member of our youth group burst into my office, threw down his books, and screamed, "No one listens to me! My parents don't listen! My friends don't listen! All they want to do is tell me what to do! No one listens!" For the next hour I tried to do for this young person the one thing that he said no one ever did: I listened. At the end of the hour, a young person who had decided to run away from home before coming to my office had changed his mind and decided to go home to work on his problems with his parents. He really didn't want to run away. He was just desperate.

This young person was right: most of the time we don't listen. Pay attention the next time you hear two people talking. You probably will hear two monologues—each waiting for the other to finish without really paying attention or even caring what the other is saying. Perhaps this is why empathy, or active listening, is the most important growth factor in a helping relationship. It is foundational; everything else is built on it. If we do not listen when youth come to us, then we will not be able to help them.

Both *empathy* and *active listening* are technical terms used to describe a process through which we deliberately attend to what a person is saying and then let the person know what we have heard. In their common usage, the terms have a slightly different meaning. *Empathy* literally means "to feel with." In this sense, empathy refers to what we feel in response to another. In this chapter, however, empathy is used in a more restrictive sense to describe the process of deliberately attending to another person through active listening. Likewise, *listening* usually refers to a passive activity. Someone else is talking, and we are merely listening. Empathy, or active listening, is different. It is a skill that involves a two-step process.

Attending

The first step in the process of active listening is attending—paying close attention to what is being said. Not everything a person says is of equal importance. There is a lot of filler, extra details, and extraneous material. When the member of our youth group burst into my office and threw down his books, he had a lot to say. But all he said could have been expressed in five words: No one listens to me! As young people talk to us and share in a group, we need to be able to sort through what they are saying and to glean what is important.

In addition to gleaning what is important, we also need to "read between the lines." There is more to what a youth says than just "content." The teen in my office was saying more than "No one listens to me." He also was communicating a feeling. He was angry. Attending is being able to listen in such a way that we understand what is being said—the content—and how the person feels about it—the affect.

Communicating

However, if this is all that we do, we do not help the person to whom we are listening. If we are going to help the person, then we must say, "John, it really seems that no one listens to you, that no one cares, and that this makes you angry." This is the second step in the active listening process. After we pay careful attention to what the person says, then we communicate what we have heard.

It is important to let youth know that we have heard them—that we have heard both the content, or what they have said, and the affect, or how they feel about it. It also is important to neither take away from nor add to what they are saying. If a young person says, "I hate my parents," and we respond, "You're upset with your parents," then we've missed the point. The youth is not *upset*; the youth *hates*. If we water down what the youth has said, then we are telling the youth that we are not really listening. If a young person says, "My mom and I aren't getting along right now," and we respond, "You're angry with your mom," then we've missed the point in the other direction. The youth has not said that he or she is angry; the youth has said only that they are not getting along. The idea behind active listening is to reflect what the person has said to us as accurately as possible. This lets the person know that we're listening, that we're taking the time and the effort to pay attention to what he or she is saying.

It is amazing what happens when we take the time to listen to teenagers—not to ask questions to satisfy our own curiosity or to provide our solutions or answers, but just to listen. Simply repeating in condensed form what the young person has said can be the most powerful tool at our disposal—if we trust it. If you try to listen to a young person for a while, you will discover just how hard this is. We're programmed not to listen. After years of using this skill, I still find myself wanting to ask questions and to provide answers—anything but listen. Listening is a skill. It must be learned through practice. At first it will seem awkward and artificial, but with time and experience it will become easy. Most young people have a deep need to be heard—to be *really heard*. If we can provide youth with a place and a relationship in which they can be heard, then we are taking the first step in helping them.

The easiest way to learn the skill of listening is to practice it. Youth will pick up the skill to some degree by watching you model active listening in the group. However, it is much more effective to take the group through a short training session. You might want to do this before or during your first session. I recommend the four-step process that Barbara Varenhorst uses in *Training Teenagers for Peer Ministry* (Group Books, 1988).

1) **Begin by explaining the skill.** Let the group members know that listening involves both attending and communicating.

2) **Next, model the skill.** Choose someone who is willing to share a real problem. As he or she shares, use active listening skills to the best of your ability. Do this for five to ten minutes and then allow the group members to ask questions. Make sure they understand what you are asking them to do.

3) **Divide the group into dyads and have them role work the skill.** One person in each dyad will share an actual problem or issue that is important to him or her. The other person will practice repeating what was said. The listener is not to ask questions but is to communicate what he or she has heard. After ten minutes, have the two people in each dyad reverse roles. This will enable all of the group members to practice the skill of active listening and to experience what it is like to have someone listen to them.

4) **Debrief the experience.** Have the group members share what it was like to be the listener and what it was like to be the helper. See if they can identify what did and did not help. If the youth would like to repeat the exercise, do so. This time allow fifteen minutes for each person to share.

2. Warmth

The second factor that is important when helping young people is warmth. We show warmth when we let youth know that we genuinely care about them. Those of us who work with youth know how important this is. Our young people can tell us which teachers at school really want to be there and which ones really like them. David Stone often states that the key question youth ask of adults who work with them is "Do you like me?" When youth begin a new semester, the conversation is not about "Which class are you taking?" but "Who did you get?" Is it someone who likes teens or someone who doesn't?

The same thing is true in our relationships with adolescents. To express warmth, we have to let youth know that we really do like them—that we genuinely care about them, their world, their concerns, and their issues. When a junior high wants to go on and on about his or her latest crush, we express warmth by letting the youth know that he or she and his or her concern really are important to us.

The opposite of being warm is being cold, distant, harsh, or judgmental. These things will keep young people at a distance. Warmth invites youth into our lives, so that they can share their lives with us. Warmth is the invisible "welcome sign" we hang on our relationships.

Warmth cannot be taught. Either you care about youth or you don't. But the expression of warmth is a skill that can be refined. We always can work on ways to let young people know we care. I express warmth when I take time for teenagers, when I give a hug or a smile, and when I express an interest in a young person's activities.

If I do not genuinely care about youth—if I do not genuinely express warmth to them—then I cannot expect them to trust me or to believe that I can help them. If warmth is not present when young people come into a group, then we literally will "freeze them out." The key within the sharing group is to express warmth. We need to constantly let youth know that we care, that we're glad they are there, and that their concerns and feelings are important. It is equally important to train youth to express warmth to one another.

3. Respect

To respect a person is to accept a person for what he or she is—to accept his or her experiences and feelings for what they are. It is to suspend all critical judgment. The comedian Rodney Dangerfield has built a career on the comment that he "gets no respect." Most of today's young people can identify with that feeling. They get little respect. They are not adults. Their opinions and views carry little weight. Few people really take the time to listen to them.

As we work with youth in sharing groups, we need to respect them, their experiences, their feelings, and their thoughts. If a young person in the group says, "I hate my dad!" we may be tempted to say something such as, "You don't really hate your dad; you're just angry with your dad because he grounded you." Sometimes we're uncomfortable with the things youth say. Youth can be very blunt. They have thoughts and feelings that we may find disturbing. It is disturbing to many of us to hear a young person say, "I hate God," or "I hate the church," or "I'm an atheist," or "Your youth program stinks." But if we're going to work with teenagers, we have to acknowledge that, at times, they think and feel these things and need to express them. They may not feel the same way or have the same belief a week later, but right now that is honestly where they are. To work with youth effectively, we have to respect that.

To respect someone does not mean that we have to accept everything about a person. We do not have to accept behavior or values. Some behavior is unacceptable. If a member of the group starts to hit another member, that behavior needs to be stopped. We do not have to respect an act of violence, nor do we have to respect values. Some values are simply unacceptable. Racial slurs, put downs, and the values behind them are also unacceptable. We can let young people know that certain values and behaviors are unacceptable as long as we also let them know that we still respect them as people. We respect their thoughts, their feelings, and their experiences. We show this respect when we accept the fact that what they are saying has meaning for them. I may see it differently, but I respect the fact that they see it that way.

We can let young people know that we hear and respect what they are saying without telling them that we agree. For example, a member of our youth group, Sam, was upset with his brother, whom he thought was an idiot. I knew Sam's brother and did not share that opinion, but I knew that Sam really believed at that moment that it was true. I needed to let Sam know that I heard him and respected his experience but that I did not share his view of his brother. I said, "Sam, you think your brother is an idiot and you're frustrated with him because. . . ." Not only is it important to respect what youth say, but it also is important to remain objective. We need to avoid collusion, or "buying into" the way that others see things. When I said to Sam "you think," I was telling him that I heard him but that it was his opinion of his brother rather than my opinion.

Youth need respect. They get tired of being told what they do or do not think, feel, and experience. As we talk with them in our groups, we can let them know that we respect what they are saying. We can let them know that there is at least one place where their experiences, thoughts, and feelings not only will be heard but also will be respected.

4. Concreteness

Many youth and adults have the ability to talk for a long time without getting to the point. They can get lost in "the story" without ever getting to the real issue. They can drown the listener in countless details, most of which have little to do with what is important. We can't help a young person as long as his or her sharing is general or vague. If we can't figure out what someone is talking about, then chances are that he or she can't either. Often young people are vague to avoid a painful issue or experience. Young people can avoid the pain by talking around the issue or by being so general that what they are saying is almost insignificant.

The only way that a young person can deal with a problem in the sharing group setting is to be specific and concrete. A young person does this by sharing details, examples, specific incidents, and feelings. If you're not sure what the person is saying, ask for examples and details. A girl in one of our groups was upset because she thought her friend was a jerk. After several minutes of sharing, all that was clear to the group was that she was angry with her friend and wanted to call the friend names. When another member of the group said that he was not sure why Nancy thought her friend was a jerk, Nancy told us about a time when her friend—who was warm and affectionate when just the two of them were together at church—walked away from her at school when other people were around. As she shared this incident, Nancy began to cry. It was clear that her anger was covering up a lot of hurt.

Sharing specific incidents and examples helps youth to express their true feelings. Encouraging young people to be specific helps them come to terms with what is going on in their lives. We need to invite youth to tell us what is going on in their lives. We can help them only if we know exactly what happened and how they are dealing with the experience.

5. Genuineness

Being genuine is being honest and being yourself—not being fake or phony. It also is being spontaneous and unrehearsed. All of these things are essential in a helping environment.

In youth programs at our church, we sometimes talk about how youth wear "masks." They do this by carefully shaping how others perceive them. The young people in our youth group often say that they cannot be themselves at school. They have to edit or censor or pretend just to be accepted. Only at church can they "be themselves." All of us need a place where we can let the mask drop—a place where we can just be ourselves.

To be genuine in a sharing group means that we make no pretense. In other words, we do not have to edit or censor what we say. As long as the concern or feeling is genuine, it is not off limits. I operate in a sharing group with a slightly different set of standards than I do in other settings. We edit much of the language we use in church groups. Some language is offensive to many people. In a sharing group setting, however, a young person may use a word that many would find offensive—especially if he or she is upset. I do not encourage this, but I also do not deal with it in the same way that I would in other settings. If youth cannot be themselves in sharing groups—if they feel that there are parts of themselves that are unacceptable to the group—then they will not be able to grow. Essential to the helping environment is the freedom to be yourself without fear of being judged or rejected.

This freedom to be genuine holds true for the adult leader as well. The adult leader is a human being who has feelings, thoughts, and reactions. The adult leader can model the quality of genuineness. The group members and the adult leader need to share openly and honestly without hiding, covering up, or pretending.

6. Self-Disclosure

A person cannot talk about an issue or problem in a helpful way without talking about himself or herself. People find help when they reveal their thoughts, feelings, and experiences to others. This is what sharing is all about: disclosing yourself to another. Young people sometimes are tempted to talk about their problems without revealing anything about themselves. Self-disclosure means that only by talking about themselves—by risking the painful stuff—can members begin to heal.

At times a person may have legitimate reasons for not wanting to bring up a painful experience or a personal struggle. To talk about it brings back the pain. Some youth in our groups still avoid the pain caused by things that happened years ago—divorces, deaths, abuse, tragic experiences, and so forth. Until these youth deal with the pain, the pain always will be with them. Painful experiences are a lot like boils on the body. They tend to fester until they are lanced, and they may need to be lanced several times. Self-disclosure is an emotional lance. It hurts, but it helps. Talking about what's going on, about the experience and about his or her feelings, helps a person to work through the pain.

The group leader also can use self-disclosure. If a young person is dealing with the divorce of his or her parents and you have experienced divorce in your family, then it is appropriate for you to say, "That happened to me, too." This lets the young person know that you understand some of what he or she is going through. The key is to be brief and to the point. Also, share only if you think that it might help the person who is sharing.

Because young people sometimes identify with a problem and shift the group's focus by sharing their own stories in great detail, keep the focus on the person who is being helped. As he or she reveals what is going on, others may share—occasionally and briefly—when they have common experiences to relate. In this way, the group lets the person know that he or she is not the only one who has had that experience.

7. Immediacy

Young people love to talk about issues and experiences "there and then." That is, they want to tell the story of what happened to them. The problem is that no one can change the past. The real issue is how they are dealing with the experience "here and now," in the present moment. If a member of our group has had a painful run-in with a teacher, rehashing the incident blow by blow usually is not very helpful. What is helpful is to find out how the youth is dealing with the incident right now. This is called immediacy.

As the group members begin to share, we need to help them process how they are doing "here and now." The person—his or her experience and feelings—is more important than the story, or what happened. Young people often tell a story dispassionately, but their feelings surface when we invite them to share how they are doing *right now*. The ability to process how they are handling an experience in the present moment is a key growth factor.

8. Confrontation

The hardest growth factor for many of us to use is confrontation. Some of us are uncomfortable with confrontation and are reluctant to use it, but we cannot help a person unless we are willing to be honest. It is not helpful to let everything go unchallenged or slide by without comment. One of the greatest assets of a group is the ability of group members to see things in us that we cannot see in ourselves. At times we need to be confronted with these perceptions.

In his book *Do You Care? Compassion in the Sunday School*, Duane Ewers refers to this kind of activity as *carefronting*.[2] Confrontation is a form of care. If we genuinely care about a person, then we will take the time and effort to confront things that might be harmful.

Confrontation as a growth factor is different from confrontation as it usually is understood. Confrontation in a sharing group is not an attack. Attacks begin with the word *you* and end with name calling: "You are sick," "You are weird," and so forth. Because adolescents do a lot of attacking, the kind of confrontation experienced in the sharing group will be new to many of them. This kind of confrontation happens when one person sees a discrepancy in another and shares that awareness with the person. An attack makes a statement about a person, whereas confrontation makes a statement about something observable—a behavior or remark. An attack is uninvited, whereas confrontation is both invited and accepted. When a person enters a sharing group, he or she agrees to listen to other people's perceptions of himself or herself. The person does not, however, agree to be attacked.

Three kinds of confrontation are helpful in a sharing group.

● The first kind is the easiest kind for a person to handle. When a member of a group says one thing and later says the opposite, it may be helpful for that person to hear the two comments one after the other. For example, a member of one of our groups told us how much he hated his sister. A few minutes later he told us about how much he loved his sister. Another member suddenly said, "I'm confused! First you said you hated your sister, but now you say you love her." This came as a revelation to the person who was sharing and helped him to realize that he had both feelings.

• A second form of confrontation involves pointing out a discrepancy between what a person says and does. On one occasion, a person in our group said that he cared about the members of the group, that he trusted them, and that he thought of them as close friends. When members of the group pointed out that he never had shared anything even remotely personal or made any attempt to have contact with them outside the group, he was shocked. This helped him to learn something valuable about himself.

• A third level of confrontation involves pointing out the discrepancy between a person's self-perception and the way that others perceive him or her. A group member who is sitting outside the circle with his or her arms crossed may say that he or she feels comfortable and at home in the group, but the person's body language says something different. Pointing out the discrepancy between the two perceptions can be helpful. More will be said about this form of confrontation in chapter 10. The first two forms of confrontation are used primarily in a sharing group.

* * *

These eight growth factors involve things that all of us can do. They may seem awkward at first and they may require practice, but they are within our reach. If we can incorporate these factors in our groups and in our ministries, then we can help youth and assist them in helping one another.

REFLECTION QUESTIONS

1. What is your reaction to Carkhuff's findings? Did his conclusions surprise you?
2. Which of the growth factors would be easiest for you to use? Which would be most difficult?
3. Think of some natural helpers you have known. What made them helpful?

TRAINING TOOLS

1. Practice giving empathetic responses in dyads. Have one person be the sharer and the other person be the helper. Talk about a real issue for ten minutes. As the sharer shares, the helper uses active listening to let the person know that he or she has heard what has been said. The helper is not to ask questions or to make comments but is only to reflect what he or she hears the person saying. After ten minutes, the two trade roles. Afterward, process the experience using the following questions:

   When you were sharing, what let you know that your partner really heard you?
   When you were listening, what was the most difficult thing to do? Did you find yourself wanting to ask questions or give solutions?

2. Define each of the eight growth factors and have the group suggest responses that reflect each of the growth factors. Why is each factor important to helping people?

Twelve Covenant
Guidelines for Sharing Groups

The Christian community is based on covenant relationships. The community itself exists because of the covenant between God and the human race and because of the covenants among the members of the community. A *covenant* is an agreement. It expresses what we will give and what we will receive within a particular relationship. Sharing groups are also covenant communities. They exist because of the covenants that the members make with one another.

Within the sharing group, the members agree to create a special relationship that rarely exists in the world. They agree to create a helping environment in which the members can trust, share, and grow. They agree to work together toward a common goal and to be intentional in reaching that goal. That goal is growth or wholeness. If a sharing group cannot agree to follow some basic guidelines, then it will be unable to create an atmosphere in which people can grow. If, however, the group members can agree to covenant with one another to achieve growth and wholeness, then they will have cleared the biggest hurdle.

Carefully review the twelve guidelines in this chapter with your group to make sure that they understand each guideline and why it is important. The group members need to understand that they are creating a special environment in which trust can be developed and in which people can share. Youth are aware that these things usually do not happen at school or in many of their relationships with peers. If the youth are to have a group in which they can share significant parts of their lives, however, they must be willing to do things differently than they normally do. Therefore, if they understand why the guidelines are necessary, they will be more committed to them and more inclined to work with you in maintaining the group structure. Appendix B contains a list of the twelve covenants for sharing groups which you can photocopy and hand out to the young people.

1. Regular Attendance

Sharon met with me earlier in the week and mentioned that she finally was ready to talk about her parents' divorce in the sharing group session. It had taken a lot of time to do it, but she had built her trust to the point that she was willing to talk about a very painful part of her life. When Wednesday night came and the sharing group gathered, Sharon began to talk. Just as she started, Tom, who had not been there for several weeks, came in and sat down. Sharon immediately froze and refused to say another word. Later, when I asked her what happened, she said that she trusted the group but that she did not trust Tom. She added, "He doesn't really care. He only drops in when it's convenient."

It is disruptive when people are constantly coming and going in a group. Sharon's experience is not unusual. When a person joins a sharing group, that person is making a commitment to be there week after week.

On another occasion, Chris finally had worked up her courage to deal with a painful experience. She needed the support of the group. She needed Jenny's help, in particular. Jenny was the one person whom Chris thought would understand. On the night that Chris was going to share, Jenny was not able to be there. Because Jenny was not present and could not give Chris the support that she needed, Chris could not bring herself to risk sharing that night.

Group members need to understand how significant each member is to the group. If even one member is missing, the group chemistry changes. From time to time, members will need to miss a session. This is understandable. But these instances need to be rare exceptions. All group members need to commit to regular attendance. They also need to commit to arriving on time and to staying until the set ending time—week after week. When members make this kind of commitment, they begin to trust one another with significant parts of their lives. If youth cannot make this commitment, the group usually dies within two or three months.

When a new group begins, allow the members two or three weeks to "check it out"—to see if they are really interested. After this period, close the group to new members for a predetermined period of time. This lets the group members know that there will not be a continual flow of people in and out of the group. It also lets them know who has made the commitment to be in the group and whom they can trust. The group can be opened to new members several times a year, or new groups can be started periodically. We usually open our groups to new members three times a year: at the beginning of the fall and spring semesters and at the beginning of the summer.

Occasionally, you may become aware of a person who really needs a sharing group and does not need to wait until one opens. If this happens, share the information with the group and ask them if it is all right to allow this person to join the group. Bringing a new person into the group affects everyone in the group, and the group members have the right to make the final decision.

Once, I brought a new member into the group without first checking with the group. They were polite and friendly to the new person. Then, after the session, several members shared their resentment that I would bring a new member into the group without first checking with them. They were angry that I thought it was my group rather than theirs.

I never have had a group to turn down a request to bring a new person into the group. They understand that special needs can arise, and they know that I would not make the request unless someone was having a crisis. But group members do want to be consulted. They understandably want to know that their opinions and feelings are important.

2. Willingness to Share

Several years ago I formed a sharing group that died after its first session. When we gathered for the first meeting, no one was willing to share. When I asked the group members why they were there, each gave the same answer: they were there "to help other people with their problems." No one was willing to talk about his or her own life and experiences. They were there to be junior therapists.

During the past few years, I have learned some techniques that might have saved that group. These are listed in chapter 10. The point to be made here is this: without sharing, there is no sharing group. Unless we are willing to talk about our own lives, our struggles, our joys, and our pain, the group cannot exist. There are no observers in a sharing group; there are only participants.

When young people join a sharing group, not only are they committing themselves to be present, but they also are committing themselves to share their lives with the other members of the group. This involves a considerable risk on the individual's part. The group does not have to begin its first session by sharing heavy issues, but it does need to begin by sharing. The members need to understand why the group exists. When they come, they come to share.

The group actually becomes a group the first time that a member shares something significant. By *significant* I mean something that stirs emotions: sadness, fear, anger, guilt, and so forth. It is easy to not pay attention and to not take the group seriously until the first person is willing to open up and be honest about something real and important in his or her life—something that stirs the emotions. At that point, the horseplay stops, the group members become focused, and the group jells. As young people are willing to trust one another and share with one another, the group will grow close. Each time that sharing takes place, the group members are bonded closer together.

Just as the group becomes a group when the first person shares something significant, so also each person in the group becomes a member of the group when he or she first shares his or her life with the other members. The members who share feel as if they belong, as if the group is *theirs*. The members who do not share tend to feel like outsiders. When a young person is willing to claim some of the group's time, to share

44

something important and to have the group focus its attention on him or her, something wonderful happens: that person belongs.

Erik almost left his sharing group after two months. Week after week Erik sat in the group and never shared anything personal. He was friendly, he was outgoing, and he interacted with others, but he never let anyone see what was inside. As the weeks passed, Erik began to withdraw from the group. He sat at the edge and began to interact less and less. When someone pointed this out to him in a session, he confided that he really didn't feel like a part of the group. He couldn't see what "the big deal" was or why the other members seemed to get so much from the sessions when he did not. Someone asked Erik if he felt this way only in this group or if he felt this way in other areas of his life. For the next hour and a half, Erik told the group how hard it was for him to share anything personal, how much he wanted to belong, and how lonely he felt. At the end of the session, Erik commented that for the first time in years he felt that he belonged and that there were people who really cared.

This does not mean that each member has to have a "problem" to share each week. It does mean that each member must be willing to share important issues when such issues arise. It also means that the group members must be willing to interact with the person who is sharing. As Jim shares that he is failing in school, the other members interact with him. Some share their own fears of failing, some share their concern, some share their love, some offer their help in tutoring, and one just holds Jim's hand. Each person interacts differently, but all share in their own ways as Jim deals with his pain.

3. Focus on the Person Who Is Sharing

When a group member finally is willing to open up and share, the task of the group is to listen and to try to understand the person's experience and feelings. When someone claims time, it is *their time.* They have the floor and should have the group's undivided attention. The group should avoid doing or saying anything that shifts the focus from the person who is sharing.

This is often hard for young people to do. Each has a need to talk and to be heard. When one person is sharing, it is very common for another to say, "Oh, that happened to me, too," and then begin to tell the story in great detail. Sometimes it seems that members are playing a game of "I can top that one . . . let me tell you what happened to me." If this happens, call attention to what is going on and then gently return the attention of the group to the person who is sharing. Another technique is to continue looking at the person who is

sharing and to address your comments to him or her. This will keep the attention of the group on the person who is sharing. Occasionally, you may have to remind a person who is grandstanding of the sharing process and of this covenant—to focus on the person who is sharing. Members should relate comments and examples only if they will help the person who is sharing. Even then, comments should be brief. If all the heads in the group turn to the new speaker and remain focused on him or her for more than a few seconds, then the group is not helping the individual who was sharing. When this happens, refocus the group's attention on the person who has claimed time. If Joe was talking and Mark tries to steal the group's attention, simply continue to look at Joe and then cut Mark off as gently as possible by saying something such as, "Joe, what do you hear Mark saying to you?" This returns the attention to Joe, but it also affirms that Mark was saying something to help Joe. The group needs to understand that focusing on the person who is sharing is crucial. If you model this, then the youth gradually will pick it up and begin to help.

There are other destructive ways that group members steal the attention from the person who is sharing. Having side conversations, making flippant comments, and leaving the room disrupt what is going on in the group. Members need to know that the person who is sharing perceives all of these things as signs that an individual does not care. Care is expressed by intentionally focusing on the person and on what he or she is saying.

4. The Person Is More Important than the Story

At camp a few years ago, a girl from another church claimed some time in our sharing group. After she shared for several minutes, I realized that she wasn't saying anything about herself. She was narrating a long story that could have gone on for hours. I stopped her and told her that I did not hear anything personal in what she was saying. She became angry and insisted that it was important for us to have "all the facts." I took a risk by telling her that I did not think we needed all the facts and that we probably did not need to hear any more of the story. Then I told her that *she* was important, not the story. What was important were her feelings and how what happened in the story was affecting her.

For the next few seconds she was silent, and her eyes began to water. Then she began to tell us about all the pain she was experiencing. Later that week she thanked me for cutting off her story. She confided that she had told the story, with its many details, to many people and that it never had changed anything. But the first time that someone would not let her finish the story, it changed her life. It gave her a chance to face the feelings that she had been avoiding.

The person is more important than the story. We don't come to the sharing group to hear stories. We come because we care about people. You can tell the difference between a story and genuine sharing by watching the group. When someone is telling a story, the group is either tuned out and bored or busy asking dozens of "tidbit" questions. When a person is genuinely sharing, the group is tuned in and focused on what the person is sharing. Another indicator is that a person almost never expresses feelings when narrating a story. Sharing involves emotional content.

Telling a story often is a way to avoid what is important: feelings. We do young people a favor when we cut the story short and enable them to move on to the personal dimension. At times, it is important to get a few of the facts straight, so that we know what the person is dealing with. But it is surprising how little of the story we need to know in order to understand. One tear, one outburst of anger, or one vivid expression often tells us more than a fifteen-minute narration of the facts.

5. Attempt to Understand the Problem, Not to Solve It

One of the biggest temptations for group members is to provide answers or to solve the problem. Many times a person has just begun to share when another member says, "I know what you should do . . . ," or, "If I were you, I would . . . ," or "Why don't you. . . . " When this happens, the person who is sharing usually stops talking and withdraws. Giving solutions or answers almost always is harmful, especially when a person has just begun to share.

Providing our answers to other people's problems is dangerous for several reasons.

● First, other people really don't want our answers. In her book *Training Teenagers for Peer Ministry*, Barbara

Varenhorst includes a wonderful exercise called "The Decision Agent" which reminds teenagers that none of us really wants other people's answers. We want to find our own solutions.[1]

One of the youth in our sharing group was sharing something important when another member cut her off to offer his solution. She gave him a look that could kill and then said, "I don't want your answers. I want you to listen to me!" Blunt, but effective.

Even when people specifically ask for advice, they usually don't want it. Try this experiment: the next time a person asks you what to do, *tell* him or her. Give your best solution. Most of the time you will hear something such as, "Yes, but . . . ," which means, "Yes, I hear you, but I really don't want to take your advice." The reason for this response is that our answer probably is not their answer. The request "What should I do?" almost always is a veiled way of asking us to listen. My response to a request for a solution is to say something such as, "I don't know. What do you think you should do?" If the person really wants your opinion, and occasionally he or she does, then he or she will make the request again. If the person does not make the request again, then he or she just wants you to listen.

After school one day, a youth who was extremely upset came by my office. She felt that her home situation was intolerable, and she had made the decision to leave home. She didn't want me to talk her out of it. All she wanted was my advice on where she could go. It took a lot of restraint for me not to take the bait. But instead of giving her what she asked for, I asked her what had happened. I spent the next two hours listening to her pour out her pain and her frustration. Afterward, she decided—on her own—that she really didn't want to move out but that she needed to talk to her parents. When I asked why she had come to me for "advice," she said that it was because she knew I wouldn't give it. She asked me for the names of homes where she could go, hoping that I wouldn't give them to her.

• A second reason for not giving solutions is even more important than the first reason: it cuts people off. To give someone an answer is to say, "I'm finished listening. Here's what you should do." Often a person will talk a while before getting to the real issue or to a feeling level. Professional counselors speak of the difference between the *presenting issue* and the *real issue.* When we prematurely cut off a person by giving an answer, we may prevent the person from ever dealing with the real problem.

The first time Jill talked about her mother's death, she began by talking about her school, her friends, and how lonely she was. After she had talked for nearly twenty minutes about these very real issues, someone asked if she was lonely only at school. At that point she began to sob and to talk about how much she missed her mother. This was the first time in the four years since her mother had been killed that she really had dealt with the pain and loneliness. If any of us had provided an answer to the school problems during the first twenty minutes, then we would have missed Jill's real issue.

• A third reason to avoid giving solutions is that often there are no answers. Young people face situations that we often are powerless to change. Sometimes young people face issues that even they are powerless to change. When Mom and Dad are getting a divorce, there may be very little that the youth or anyone else can do. But what we can do is listen and let the youth know that we care. This may seem to be of little help, but often this is "the answer." Just being heard and cared for helps the teen to cope with the situation. As much as we would like to, we can't solve other people's problems for them. However, we can provide love and support.

Occasionally it is appropriate to look for solutions together. Sometimes youth need to make difficult decisions; they need answers. Listening is not enough. If you have listened carefully and the person really does need an answer, then the group can help. Together they can brainstorm alternatives. The group could role play possible options or use a decision-making model, such as the one in David Stone's *Friend To Friend: How You Can Help a Friend Through a Problem,* to help the person make a decision.[2] The key is that the answer must be the individual's answer, not our answer. The group can give options or ideas, but only the individual can choose an answer. If you are not sure whether to listen or to go on to problem solving, then remember that it is safer to err on the side of listening.

6. Use the Eight Growth Factors

It is important for everyone in the group to understand and use the eight growth factors presented in chapter 5. The group will need to be constantly reminded of these growth factors for the first several weeks. If a growth factor is violated, gently and lovingly point it out to the individual by saying something such as,

"Bill, I know you don't see it the way Jim does, but it's important that we respect the fact that he does see it that way." As the group leader, it is your responsibility to call fouls and to redirect the group to the ground rules. If we role model this process, then the young people will pick up on it and become guardians of the growth factors.

My sharing group has been together for three years, and it has been over a year since I have had to remind them of a growth factor. The group members do that for one another. When new members come into the group, the other members "train" them and remind them of what is important.

7. Allow Time for Silence

There are times when the most helpful thing that we can do for a person who is sharing is to allow time for silence. Most of us are uncomfortable with silence, so we try to fill the silence with our observations or questions. Many times a person needs a time of silence. Silence can be extremely productive. If we have asked someone a question, then he or she may need time to think about an answer. The person also may need time to allow feelings to surface. We do someone a disservice when we fill the silence with our chatter or questions. The focus always should be on the person who is sharing—on his or her concerns and needs. We need to learn how to use silence rather than avoid it.

If Jeff is sharing and then suddenly becomes quiet, this does not mean that I need to say something to get him to talk again. It means that something is going on inside Jeff—something important. Waiting thirty seconds to a minute may help Jeff to get in touch with his feelings or to formulate what he is about to say. By respecting Jeff's silence, I am applying a healthy pressure on him to continue to process what is going on inside. If I speak or ask a question, I give him an excuse to ignore his feelings while he responds or answers my question.

8. Keep Information Confidential

Twice in the last seven years one of our sharing groups died because of a break in confidentiality. There are no guidelines more important than this one. What is said in the group stays in the room. The surest way to destroy the group is to violate this guideline. If the members of your group are not absolutely certain that what they share will be held in confidence, then they will not share anything of consequence. Someone who cannot keep a confidence should not be in a sharing group.

It is impossible to know what another person might be sensitive about. Sometimes a group member shares something with someone outside the group, honestly believing that what he or she has shared is not confidential. I have even done this myself.

One of the worst crises in our sharing group happened four years ago when I unknowingly broke confidentiality. A group member had spent more than an hour telling us about what a hard time she was having. She was overwhelmed by a variety of things, and she was at her breaking point. Later that evening when her parents were leaving a church meeting, they shared with me that they were going to have to "come down hard" on their daughter about her schoolwork and her untidy room. I suggested that they might want to wait because their daughter had had a hard day. I gave no details. The parents went home and confronted their daughter about why she was having problems and why she would not talk to them. Six months later I learned that she had dropped out of our sharing group because I had broken confidentiality. I also had to deal with the anger of other members in the group who felt the same way. The best policy is to assume that everything said in a group is confidential.

Some may wonder if youth are even capable of keeping something confidential. The answer is an emphatic yes! I know of several groups that have existed for two or three years without a break in confidentiality. Members become committed to their groups. They value what they have so much that they never would risk losing it.

Young people are smart enough to know that any break in confidentiality will get back to the group. He will tell a friend, who will tell a friend, who will tell a friend, who will tell someone in the group. This happens all the time to young people at school. They are very sensitive to the issue of confidentiality. Even seventh graders can keep things confidential. However, if you are going to have a problem with confidentiality, it usually will happen in the first few weeks—before the members become bonded to one another and to the group.

There are two primary exceptions to the confidentiality guideline.

• One exception is when an individual in the group chooses to share with someone outside the group what he or she has said about himself or herself. This was pointed out to me a few weeks ago when an irate mother called me to ask "what in the world was going on in that sharing group." Her daughter had mentioned that she had talked about herself in the group session but that she was unable to tell her mother any of the details because it was confidential.[3] Apparently, we had communicated the point of confidentiality a little too well! Of course, confidentiality applies only to what others say. We are free to tell anyone what we say about ourselves.

• A second exception involves life-threatening situations. If keeping something confidential might result in the injury or death of an individual, then confidentiality becomes of secondary importance. If a person is suicidal, for example, we cannot play into the suicide by keeping that information confidential. We should break confidence and get the person professional help. A report of child abuse is another instance when confidentiality should be broken. Although most states encourage everyone to report child abuse, many states *require* pastors and those engaged in pastoral care and counseling, which includes youth leaders and sharing group leaders, to report child abuse.[4] It is the responsibility of the sharing group leader to become familiar with state laws pertaining to such matters. The important thing is to carefully explain your confidentiality policy to the youth and to reassure them that the individual is the only one who has the right to share confidential information about himself or herself unless the situation is life threatening or the law requires that confidentiality be broken.[5]

9. Do Not Attack Others

Sometimes young people blame others for their problems. You may hear something such as "they did this or that to me." Usually, guideline number four—the person is more important than the story—covers this. Occasionally, however, group members will attack another person in or out of the group. When this happens, affirm that anger and the expression of anger are all right, but that attacking or putting down another person is not all right. Then be sure to communicate the difference between the two.

Name calling does not help a person in need. What does help is expressing and dealing with feelings. The best way to do this without attacking others is to encourage the use of "I statements." Encourage Peter to say "I'm angry at Jack because . . . " rather than "Jack's a jerk!" The first statement helps Peter come to terms with his anger. The second statement turns the sharing group into a gripe session or a pity party.

Sometimes an attack can be disguised as an "I statement," such as "I feel that Jack is a Jerk" or "I'm angry at Jack because he's a jerk!" The difference between dealing with anger in a healthy way and attacking another person is the person's focal point. To deal with anger in a healthy way, the person sharing should focus on himself or herself rather than on another person. If another person is mentioned, the statement should relate to specific, observable behavior, such as "When Jack ignores me or puts me down, I get angry."

10. Do Not Talk About Members Who Are Not Present

When I first started working with sharing groups, a conflict emerged between two members of our group. At one session, Andrea was angry at Valery, who happened to be absent that night. Andrea spent an hour talking about her relationship with Valery and how painful their conflict was. The group made sure that Andrea used "I statements," and there was a minimum of attacks on Valery.

When Valery returned the next week and discovered that Andrea had spent an hour talking about their relationship, she was furious. Her reaction precipitated a crisis in the group which resulted in the addition of a new guideline: do not talk about members who are not present. The new guideline meant that whenever Andrea or anyone else wanted to deal with an issue involving another member, she or he would have to wait until that member was present. It also meant that the individual who wanted to share would have to get the other person's permission to deal with their relationship in the group. Subsequent experience has underscored the wisdom of this guideline. People do not want others to talk about them when they are not there—with or without "I statements."

11. Avoid Using Names When Talking About People Who Are Not in the Group

It is best not to use names when talking about situations that involve other people. Supplying names only invites others into the story. It really does not matter who the others are. What is important is how the person who is sharing is dealing with the situation. Sometimes it is impossible to keep identities secret, especially if the involved parties are members of a person's family or have a known relationship with the person. However, whenever possible, avoid becoming sidetracked by who is involved.

12. Trust Yourself and the Group

A sharing group helps a person only as long as he or she can trust others. Trust does not develop overnight. It builds slowly over time. Some adolescents find it harder to trust than others. It will take these youth longer to learn to trust. Trust also involves risk. Opening up to a group is scary. There is no way to remove the risk. You can minimize the risk by making the group a safe place in which to share, but sharing still will be scary. Opening up in a group is a lot like jumping off a diving board for the first time. Sooner or later, you just have to jump. The more you jump off the board, or share in a group, the easier it becomes.

* * *

Each of these twelve covenants serves the same purpose. All are ways to keep your group on track. They help the group to focus on its purpose, which is to give support to one another by intentionally focusing on each person as he or she shares experiences and feelings.

Sharing groups have a limited amount of time to do this, usually one-and-a-half to two hours each week. What happens during this time becomes precious to members because they often get something from the group that they can get nowhere else. This makes the time priceless. There is rarely enough time, even if time is used wisely. Anything that wastes time or distracts the group from its task should be avoided.

I have found that young people easily can understand all of the guidelines. Once the youth understand the guidelines, they are firmly committed to each one. In the end, the youth are the ones who gain if genuine sharing takes place—and they are the ones who lose if it doesn't.

REFLECTION QUESTIONS

1. Which of the guidelines do you consider to be most important?
2. What guidelines would you add to the list to help the group in its task?
3. What attendance guidelines would you use with a group? Why? Would you make exceptions? If so, under what conditions?
4. How would you deal with a break in confidentiality?

TRAINING TOOLS

1. Review the guidelines with your group and discuss each one. Do they understand the guideline? Do they understand why the guideline is important?
2. Have the group brainstorm ways that a leader can deal with a person who wants to tell a story without sharing anything personal.
3. Have the group discuss confidentiality. How would they deal with a break in confidentiality? Under what conditions would they break confidentiality?

Twelve Tools
for Sharing Groups

When I first entered youth ministry, I was terrified. I didn't know what to do. Every dimension of youth ministry seemed overwhelming. I had to learn how to teach a class, plan a program, counsel young people, lead recreation, work with parents, plan worship, recruit and train volunteers—the list goes on and on. After several years in youth ministry, I could approach each of these dimensions of youth ministry with some level of comfort. What made the difference was having the right tools and techniques, or tricks of the trade—things I could do in each of these situations that would work. Some of these tools I gleaned from books, many of them I learned from other youth ministers, and a few of them I discovered on my own.

There also are tools for the sharing group. When I meet with an existing group or start a new group, I know what to expect. I have a fair idea of what will and will not work. I know some things to do to facilitate the group and a few things to avoid. After comparing experiences with several others who have led sharing groups, I have compiled a working list of basic tools that can be used in the sharing group format. Most of these are not formal counseling techniques, but all of them are tools that any good counselor would use.

Once we understand what kind of environment helps people to grow and how to provide a basic structure to make sharing possible, we need to know a few basic techniques to help the group members share their experiences. The twelve tools in this chapter are not definitive; rather, they are only some of the things that those of us who work with sharing groups have found to be particularly helpful. You may want to compare this list with lists in other resources. One such list can be found in Keith Olson's *Counseling Teenagers*.[1]

1. Begin and End with Prayer

The period just before our group begins is usually a rowdy time. Everyone is hyper and glad to see one another. Tina shows us her new drill routine. Julie and Sara share a note that one of them received at school. Bill does his homework. Then the magic words come: "Let's pray." Suddenly, we all link hands, bow our heads, and become focused.

This is not a fantasy or a portrait of perfection; it is just a typical week in our sharing group. We begin and end with prayer. Over the years, I have found that this is the most helpful way to open and close a group. We are a church, and we do not have to be apologetic about the religious dimension of the sharing group. All that we do, we do in God's name and in God's presence. We invite God to be a part of all that goes on in the group. We lift our joys and our concerns to God. We are not just any group; we are a group of Christian believers.

On a practical level, our opening prayer makes a transition. It says to the group that we are beginning and that it is time to get serious and to focus on what we are doing. Prayer sets the tone for what follows. Our group usually has a circle prayer. As we go around the circle, each person has the opportunity to lift up whatever is on his or her heart. Some squeeze the hand next to them and pass, but most join in the prayer. As we pray, I listen for issues. Often youth will lift to God the things that they are struggling with in their lives.

As we end the session, we use the closing prayer as a way of lifting to God all that has happened. We usually have another circle prayer or ask one member to pray. The closing prayer briefly touches on all the concerns raised during the session. We invite God's healing power into our pain. Opening and closing with prayer gives the session a different feel. Praying helps us in our task of being there for one another.

2. Start with Highs and Lows

A couple of years ago, I received a call from a youth worker who was upset. After reading an article that I had written about how to set up and lead sharing groups, he had decided that starting a sharing group was a good idea for his church. He had put his group together carefully, but no one was willing to talk at the first session. He called to find out what to do before the second session. I asked him if he had tried "highs and lows." He had never heard of it.

"Highs and lows" is an essential tool. I use it in every session. Before the actual sharing begins, we take several minutes to share our highs and lows of the week—the good and bad things that have happened to us. When we first started our group, we would go around the circle. Now we just let everyone share until all the joys and concerns have been expressed. This has become a ritual for our group. The young people expect it and look forward to it. On several occasions when time was running short, I tried to get the group to skip highs and lows, but they wouldn't consider it. It means that much to them.

Sharing highs and lows accomplishes several things. First, it gets everyone to share at a very low threat level. It breaks the ice and gets everyone used to talking. The sharing of significant events in their lives begins with highs and lows. Second, it gives the leader clues about a possible agenda. When I lead a group, I am particularly interested in the lows, because these topics "clue me in" to the importance of what is being shared. The level of feeling indicates how important the topic is. After we have shared highs and lows, I usually know of half-a-dozen things that can be dealt with.

Sometimes a low can be disguised as a high. Once, a member of our group joyfully announced, "I've got a high: my parents are getting divorced." No one in the group thought that this was funny. We knew that this young person really was upset and probably needed to discuss the problem in the group.

I often follow the highs and lows by asking a group member if he or she is willing to talk about a concern. The person can say no, but usually he or she says yes. Just by bringing up the concern, the youth is indicating his or her willingness to deal with the issue on some level.

3. Use Active Listening

Although empathy was discussed in chapter 5 as a growth factor, we should remember that empathy is the most powerful tool at our disposal. Begin by listening, end with listening, and, if all else fails, listen. Continue to repeat as accurately as you can what you hear the youth saying.

There is no way to overemphasize the value of active listening. Most of my problems in sharing groups have occurred when I have tried to use some other technique at the expense of listening. Week in and week out, you will find that your ability or inability to listen will determine what happens in the group. Trust the value of listening. Avoid making comments and asking questions as much as possible. Let the members know that you really do hear what they are saying. If you are involved in using some other technique and something goes wrong, go back to your basic tool: listen.

4. Know When to Ask the Right Questions

Sam sat there looking at me. He was upset and needed to talk, but he didn't know where to begin. The painful expression on his face was pleading, "Help me; help me put it into words." There are times when we need to help youth by asking the right questions, particularly when we are helping them to share. To help youth to share, we need to ask open-ended, "feeling" questions.

All questions are either closed or open-ended. A closed question requires a yes or no answer or a short response: "Are you angry?" "Yes!" "Why did your parents ground you?" "I don't know!" Closed questions make it easy for a person not to share. An open-ended question, on the other hand, invites a person to share, because it is a question that is difficult to answer with a short response. "What's that like for you?" is an open-ended question. It invites the person to share in detail. Sometimes it is helpful to reword a question as a statement. If I ask, "Would you share what happened?" the person might respond, "No!" But if I rephrase the question and say, "Tom, share what happened to you," he is more likely to share. He still can say no, but it is more difficult.

All questions also are either content questions or feeling questions. A content question asks for data: "What happened?" "He hit me!" A feeling question asks how the person is dealing with the data: "How do you feel about what happened?" "It made me mad!" As a general rule of thumb, feeling questions are preferable. It is helpful to ask a mixture of open-ended content and open-ended feeling questions. These questions invite the person to share his or her experience with us.

The timing of questions is also important. If someone asks a person a question, then the person needs time to answer. Sometimes a group is so eager to help that they bombard the person with questions. In one of our sessions, Ted had begun to talk about ending a long relationship. When he reached an impasse, the group asked him more questions than he ever could have answered. He bent over, put his hands over his head, and screamed. We got the point. A person can answer only one question at a time. If the group asks a person a question, then they need to refrain from asking other questions until the person has had a chance to process the first one.

If a person is expressing feelings, then a content question is likely to end his or her sharing. A question that requires thinking invites the person out of his or her feelings and into his or her head. If this happens, you may want to override the question for the sake of the person. Content questions are more helpful at the beginning and end of a person's sharing. At the beginning, a content question is less threatening than a feeling question and may help the person begin to share. Once the sharing has begun, a feeling question is easier to handle. At the end of a person's sharing time, content questions can help the person to move out of deep feelings and to get ready to leave the session. If time is running out and you sense that the person is still upset, you may want to ask a content question such as, "Tom, what are you going to do about this when you get home?" This invites Tom out of his feelings and into his head. It helps him begin to make the transition from the group to the outside world.

Use questions sparingly and carefully, but remember that sometimes an open-ended question, especially an open-ended feeling question, can be very helpful.

5. Read Body Language

Young people say a lot with their bodies. Most of them have not learned to mask their body language like adults have. If Jan is sitting outside the circle and has little eye contact, this tells me something important about her. For some reason, she has withdrawn. If Kevin is sharing and the group suddenly leans in and begins to listen more intently, this tells me that Kevin has begun to deal with something significant.

All of us know body language to some degree. If we are attentive, then we can read the group. Our ears give us information about the person who is speaking. Our eyes give us information about everyone in the room. It is important to watch for these things:

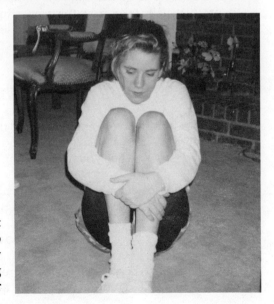

> eye contact
> facial expression (smile, frown, tears)
> physical distance
> body stance (open or closed)
> movement
> changes

All of these things can tell us a lot, if we read them.

In the group session, Maria was expressing concern about her inability to communicate with her mother. I asked her to do the chair exercise. She sat in one chair and faced an empty chair in front of her. I asked her to imagine her mother sitting in the other chair. At the mention of her mother, she dug her heals in, slid her chair back, and leaned away from the empty chair. Her body spoke in a loud volume. We spent the next thirty minutes "unpacking" her body language. Maria later said that she had not been aware of how frightened she was of her mother. Her body made her aware of her fear.

Remember that body language can be misread. A member may have his arms folded across his chest because he is cold or because it is comfortable. A lot depends on what is "normal" for that person. If you wonder about a person's body language, ask questions. Point out what you see and then ask the person to interpret his or her body language for you. The person's reaction to your question will tell you what it means. You may not believe the person—the explanation may seem weak or unconvincing. If so, you may want to share your interpretation of the person's body language. If you do this, however, acknowledge that it is your interpretation, not a fact. In the end, the person must decide what he or she will make of your observations.

6. Allow Silence

One of the least used techniques for working with youth is silence. Most of us are afraid of or uncomfortable with silence. We are quick to fill a person's silence with our own words. Ironically, silence is probably one of the best tools we have in sharing groups. Often a person needs time to think about what has been said to him or her. If we talk or ask a question, we can inhibit this valuable processing. People also need time to allow feelings to surface. Speaking or asking questions invites a person to move out of his or her feelings and into his or her head.

Jeff had begun to share but then suddenly stopped. He looked at the floor. Two of the group members started to say something, but I caught their eye and shook my head no. We sat in silence for several minutes. When Jeff looked up, tears were streaming down his face. He began to talk about how he recently had run away from home and how he felt guilty for hurting his parents. Jeff needed the silence. He needed time to come to terms with his feelings. He did not need us to fill the silence with questions or comments.

7. Allow Time

Sometimes the issue that a group member first brings up is not the real issue. A group member may be "testing the waters" to see how we handle the issue. If we take the time to listen, the member suddenly may change the subject and begin talking about the real issue. This can be an unconscious act. For example, Jill began talking about being lonely at school, but she ended up talking about how much she missed her mother and how lonely she was since her mother's death. At other times, this testing is conscious and deliberate. Young people have to be careful. They have learned that they cannot trust everyone. Often it takes time for a youth to work up to something really important.

Our group usually takes from thirty minutes to an hour-and-a-half to focus on one person's sharing. Often we use the entire session for one person. It is not unusual for us to spend the bulk of our time on an issue that is different from the one we started with. As a general rule, it takes about fifteen to twenty minutes to get to the real issue.

8. Go Where the Feelings Are

One of the youth workers in our area has three rules for adults who work with teenagers in groups: 1) go with the feelings, 2) go with the feelings, and 3) go with the feelings. He's right. The really important issues are emotional issues. When you "hit a feeling" in the process of sharing, go with it. Encourage sharing at the feeling level.

The expression of emotion is therapeutic. Anger expressed is anger drained. Tears shed are a wound lanced. Dealing with fear makes it less frightening. Sharing loneliness brings others closer to us.

9. Use Group Members' Reactions

One of the group's best resources is the group itself. The members' feelings, reactions, and comments can be extremely helpful. Group members see things that we miss. They know one another in ways that we cannot know them, and they are able to pick up on subtle clues. Their intuition can be uncanny. Over the years, I have learned to trust the group and to constantly involve them in processing what is going on in the group. As a person shares, scan the room and watch for the group members' reactions.

When Shannon was sharing something that had happened to her, I saw that Ellen, her close friend, was shaking her head no. When I asked Ellen what was going on, she began to tell Shannon why she didn't believe what she was saying. It turned out that Shannon had not been telling the truth. Because Ellen was Shannon's friend, she was in a position to help Shannon face something that she did not want to face: her manipulation of others. Encourage the group to share their feelings and reactions as someone shares. Often their observations are right.

The reactions of others also can tell us if they are dealing with a similar issue. The night Jill talked about her mother's death and how much she missed her mother, three other members began crying. Later we learned that all three had experienced a death in their families. When people share emotionally laden issues, all kinds of reactions can be set off in the group. Often we spend much of our time having the group share their reactions to something that was shared. At times this can replace the agenda that we had planned to follow. If one person's pain brings others' pain to the surface, we may find ourselves dealing with members who had no intention of claiming time but who need help.

In a group session, a member shared his pain at the loss of his father. His grief was overwhelming, and it moved the group. When he finished, I realized that several of the group members, including two adults, had been deeply affected by what he shared. It was important to take time to process their pain before we moved on to someone else's sharing.

The group's reactions are a barometer of what is going on. If they are bored, there is a reason. If they are reacting to a particular statement or feeling, their reactions need to be acknowledged and processed. These reactions are potential resources that can help the person who is sharing.

10. Avoid "Band-aiding"

The group may want to "band-aid" a problem, to prematurely provide an answer or a solution. As the group leader, you must intervene and encourage the group to continue listening. Watch for band-aiding. Often this is an indication of the person's discomfort with a topic. This can be very significant.

When Karl began to talk about his parents' separation, Marcus became agitated and tried to convince Karl to try to keep his parents together. Marcus did not want to hear any of Karl's feelings. He wanted to do everything that he could to keep Karl's mom and dad from separating. A few weeks later we learned that Marcus' parents had separated. There was a reason why Marcus was so uncomfortable with Karl's sharing. He was telling us something by trying to solve Karl's problem, but we missed it.

11. Provide Time for Closure

When each person's sharing comes to an end and when the session comes to a close, provide time for closure. It is not right to abruptly end one person's sharing and move to another, nor is it right to end a session when someone is "strung out" emotionally. We need to take a few minutes to tie up the loose ends and to make sure that the person is ready for us to move on to someone else.

Never abandon a person who is deep into his or her feelings. Take the time to help the person get himself or herself together. If a person is having difficulty getting out of his or her feelings, ask content questions to help the person to think. If a person needs more time to cry or to express a feeling, give it to him or her. Then have the group express their reactions to what has been said, and encourage the group to give support. This is especially important if a person has shared something sensitive.

Also, take time to deal with fears. A person may feel vulnerable and may worry about how the group members will react to what he or she has shared. The person wants to know if the group will have different feelings for him or her. I usually ask the person if he or she has this fear. If the person says yes, then I ask if he or she would like to know how the other members feel. Then I invite the group to share their reactions and feelings. This is a very affirming experience. When it is appropriate, encourage the members to offer one

SHARING GROUPS IN YOUTH MINISTRY

another hugs. When a person feels vulnerable or sensitive, receiving a hug from each member of the group helps to make the person feel loved and accepted.

Always ask the person who has been sharing if it is all right to move on to someone else. Occasionally a person in our group will say no, and we will spend more time with him or her. Usually, however, the answer is yes. Most youth are relieved when the attention is shifted to someone else.

The way we provide closure is just as important as the way we listen. Both can be ways of letting youth know that they are important and that we care about them.

12. Give Follow-up Support

Often the care that a youth receives in the sharing group session is all that he or she needs. Sometimes, however, the person may need follow-up care. We may want to suggest that the person contact other members in the group during the week. Members can contact one another by phone, or they can get together in person. Further contact can meet a variety of needs. A lonely person can reach out to others. People with common needs and problems can continue the work that was begun in the group.

Sara spent a part of one group session dealing with an incident of sexual abuse that happened when she was seven. One of the things she talked about was how she was afraid that no one would understand how she felt. In the course of the evening, Terri shared that she, too, had been sexually abused by a relative when she was younger. I suggested that they might want to get together outside of the group. A few weeks later, Sara told the group how much Terri's sharing had meant to her. With professional help, Terri had come to terms with what had happened to her, and she was able to use what she had learned in therapy to help Sara begin to deal with her own experience.

REFLECTION QUESTIONS

1. Which of the techniques described in this chapter would be the easiest for you to use? Which would be most difficult?
2. What are some basic techniques that you could use that are not mentioned in this chapter?
3. How comfortable are you with using silence? How do you normally react when a person is silent?
4. How would you help a group member get in touch with his or her feelings? What specific techniques would you use?
5. What would you do to provide closure as each person finishes sharing? What would you do at the end of the session? How would these closure techniques differ?
6. What are some suggestions for follow-up support that you can give to the group?

TRAINING TOOLS

1. Practice dyad sharing, with one person being the helper and the other person being the sharer. Use ten minutes of sharing time for each of the following:

       focusing on the person, not the story
       using silence

2. Add a third person to each dyad. This person is to watch for body language. Rotate so that each person in the triad can play each role. When you're finished, bring the entire group together. Have the group identify specific examples of body language. List these and discuss them.

Making Referrals

As you work with teenagers in a sharing group, a situation may arise that is beyond the ability of the group or your ability to handle. You may discover that a member is using drugs. It may come to your attention that someone is experiencing some form of ongoing abuse. You may become aware that a member is suicidal. Your love for these persons needs to be expressed in your efforts to help them get specialized help. You need to make a referral.

Know Your Limits

Terry Hershey, a national singles ministries workshop leader, uses a wonderful saying in some of his workshops. He invites his audience to repeat this statement: "I am not God, and the job is taken." This is a welcome reminder that we all need to hear. Likewise, in his book *Counseling Teenagers*, Keith Olson reminds us to watch out for the *messiah complex*. He defines this as a "false and unrealistic expectation that we ought to be able to help everyone."[1] We are not equipped to help everyone. Situations will arise that we cannot handle. This is not a sign of our failure or incompetence. Knowing when and how to make a referral is a sign of competence. We need to know our limits and what to do when we reach them.

When to Make a Referral

Making a referral is not a unilateral decision. It requires the knowledge and consent of the person who is being referred. We cannot force a person to accept a referral; we can only share the reasons why we think a referral would be helpful and do everything in our power to get the individual's cooperation. The first step in this process is knowing what conditions necessitate getting someone additional help. The warning signs or indications that a referral is appropriate or necessary will vary according to the situation. The key is always to seek the advice of a trained professional before determining whether or not to refer a youth. Although the warning signs are many, here is an abbreviated list of things to look for when considering a referral.

Psychotic Behavior

Psychotic is a clinical term. Few of us are qualified to judge whether or not an individual is psychotic. However, if a person appears to be out of touch with reality or if a person's behavior is so bizarre that it defies explanation, then we should seek professional help for the individual. The person could have a brain tumor or a brain disease. Many forms of mental illness can be treated by the medical community. Sharing groups are equipped to help people who are basically "mentally healthy." They are not equipped to deal with mental illness or brain diseases. If a person experiences confusion, disorientation, or memory loss, then he or she requires medical help.

Chemical Dependence

Drug and alcohol problems require professional help and often are signs of deeper emotional problems. A sharing group can provide supplemental support to someone who is receiving treatment, but a sharing group is not equipped to treat the problem itself.

Suicidal Tendencies

People who are suicidal need our love and support. They also need intervention—professional intervention. The forces at work in a person's life that drive him or her to consider suicide are beyond our control. Usually there are significant factors in the individual's family environment or relationships with others. Again, the sharing group can provide supplemental support but should not try to deal with the problem itself.

Sometimes we are not sure if a young person is really suicidal. Talking about suicide has become fashionable among teens. If you have any doubts, seek a professional assessment. Too much is at stake.

Violent or Dangerous Behavior

If a member of the group is violent or dangerous, or if a member poses a risk to his or her own health or the health of others, seek professional help. Most people who commit acts of violence give plenty of warning. If we can get help for these individuals before they hurt others, then we will be doing everyone a favor.

Evidence of Abuse

When a person is experiencing physical, sexual, or emotional abuse, we have an obligation to break the cycle and get him or her into a treatment program. As previously noted, many states require those engaged in pastoral care and counseling, which includes sharing group leaders, to report child abuse.[2] The group leader would be well advised to become familiar with the child abuse reporting laws of his or her state. If the obligation is not legal in all states, it is at least moral. This is especially true for physical and sexual abuse. Emotional abuse is harder to define and harder to deal with, but it is just as real.

Sometimes we become aware of abuse that occurred years ago. These cases involve experiences that entail deep trauma and lifelong consequences. Be sensitive to the need for referral in these cases. Just because the abuse is over does not mean that the effects of the abuse are over.

Eating Disorders

Teenagers, particularly girls, are prone to eating disorders. Chief among these are bulimia and anorexia nervosa. These disorders almost always are symptoms of much deeper problems involving the family. Eating disorders require extensive psychotherapy—usually family therapy. If someone in the group has an eating disorder, seek professional help.

Alcoholic or Drug Dependent Family Member(s)

Unfortunately, many young people deal with drug problems involving family members. These youth live in destructive environments over which they have little control. We can help these teen to process their feelings, but we cannot change their home environments. The tragedy is that unless the home environment is changed, the teen will continue to have more tragic interactions with the dependent family member. The teen also may function as a co-dependant, playing an unwitting role in the family member's disease. Research indicates that there is a high probability that the child of an alcoholic will experience similar difficulties as an adult. For all of these reasons, seek competent, professional help to intervene in the family system.

Other Situations

Other situations may require a referral. If a person is physically ill, he or she needs a doctor. If a person has committed a crime, legal authorities need to be contacted as well as legal counsel. The list could go on and on.

Rules of Thumb

For the purposes of a sharing group, a referral should be made when a group member needs help that you are not trained to offer. Never assume that you are capable of handling a given situation if you have not had the appropriate training or experience, and always seek the advice of a professional. In addition to these general guidelines, there are three rules of thumb to use in a group. You need to refer a youth to a professional if

1. You perceive that there is an immediate, serious risk to the individual or anyone else.
2. The person is destructive to the group or is monopolizing the group's time.
3. The person has an ongoing problem that cannot be worked out in the group and that is not getting better.

It is important to remember that, in most cases, referring someone to a professional does not mean that he or she is removed from the group. The individual receives help from a professional *in addition to* support from the sharing group. Generally, there is no reason why a person who is working with a professional in a treatment program cannot continue to participate in the sharing group. I consistently have found professionals to be supportive of the additional help.

How to Make a Referral

A referral can be a traumatic experience for the person who is being referred. The following nine-step checklist will help you to support a young person through this difficult process.

1. Build Rapport and Trust

Whether or not a young person is willing to accept a referral largely depends on your relationship with this person and the level of trust in your relationship. Many youth do not want to seek professional help. They are frightened by the prospect of going to a stranger and becoming involved in a process they do not understand. The more the young person trusts you, the more he or she will trust your suggestion to seek help.

2. Let the Person Know Why Help Is Needed

It is important to let the person know why you think a referral is necessary. The referral may be necessary to assess the problem or to obtain the help of a particular specialist or treatment program. Answer any questions the group member may have. Give him or her as much information as you can. You have reasons for believing that a referral would be helpful to a particular individual; the person needs to know what those reasons are.

3. Expect Resistance

The young person may have invested a lot in denying the problem. This is especially true when chemical dependence and abuse are involved. Expect the young person to resist the idea and to give all kinds of reasons why he or she cannot act on your suggestion to seek professional help.

4. Assure Continued Support

Let the individual know that you want to help him or her get additional support and help, not to hand him or her over to someone else. Assure the young person that your relationship and your support will continue.

5. Get the Individual's Permission

You cannot force another person to accept a referral. The individual has to make that decision. However, you can give reasons why you think a referral is necessary and urge the individual in the strongest possible terms.

6. Consult the Parents

Most youth in a church's youth program are minors in the legal custody of their parents. Therefore, parents' support is necessary for most referrals. Even so, if there is little or no support from the home, the effectiveness of a referral can be reduced significantly.

Whenever possible, enlist the support of parents. Let the parents know the reasons for the referral and what you hope the referral will accomplish. Most parents genuinely care about their children and are quick to respond when they are aware of a problem.

If you are dealing with a situation involving domestic abuse, you must decide how to handle your interaction with the family. In most states, laws require that those involved in pastoral counseling report any instance of abuse. This usually can be done without giving your name. In these cases, you may want to seek counsel on how to deal with the teen and the family from social workers or a local abuse clinic. Fortunately, most families do not fit into this category. Occasionally, however, you may encounter the problem of abuse.

7. Know to Whom to Refer the Youth

Making a referral sometimes can be like playing Russian roulette. Not all referral possibilities will be equally helpful. If you refer a youth to someone you know and trust, someone known to be competent in his or her field, then you increase the odds that the youth will receive help. Look for a professional or an organization with special training and competence in a given area. Most communities have a list of available community services. You can obtain such a list at your local library or city or county offices. In general, there are several types of organizations to which you can refer a youth in need.

Specialized Agencies. Today you can find organizations that provide services for almost every conceivable need: alcohol and drug rehabilitation programs, clinics for victims of rape and abuse, suicide counseling services, therapy programs for individuals with eating disorders—the list goes on and on. The Yellow Pages list many of these by topic.

Community Mental Health Centers. Most communities have a mental health organization or center of some kind that can provide services or refer you to someone who can help.

Private Practitioners. Psychiatrists, clinical psychologists, marriage and family counselors, and other professionals are available to work with people in the community through private practices. They are listed in the Yellow Pages.

A Pastor. If you are not sure what kind of referral to make or to whom to refer a youth, you may want to talk to a pastor. Most pastors make referrals all the time and have lists of people they respect and trust.

Someone You Know and Trust. Sometimes you know someone who has faced a similar problem and has received help within the community. Whoever helped that individual may be able to help you. If not, he or she probably can refer you to someone who can be of help.

Local Hospitals. If all else fails, seek help from your local hospitals. Most hospitals are equipped to conduct psychological assessments. They also should be able to provide you with a list of community resources and to direct you to the help that you need.

As you talk to the agencies in your community, there are several things to consider.

• First, what is the professional in question's training? Has this person been through a formal training program? Is this training recognized by other professionals in the field? Unfortunately, we live in an age in which many are self-proclaimed counselors or therapists with little or no formal training.

• A second consideration is this: is the professional in question certified? Most professional groups have a certification process by which they determine whether or not a person has met the requirements of the field. Psychiatrists are medical doctors who have done additional work in the field of psychology. Clinical psychologists have not had medical training, but they have done extensive work in psychology. They cannot prescribe medication, but they have counseling and therapy skills. Pastoral counselors have some of the same training as psychologists as well as training in theology. If you have questions about the qualifications for a particular field, call a hospital to find out what certification is required for that discipline.

• A third consideration is the professional in question's reputation. Determine how effective and helpful the professional is by asking others who know the individual or who have been to him or her for help.

8. Decide to Whom to Refer the Youth

Consult the group member and the parents to reach a decision about to whom to refer the youth. There are many things to consider: costs, insurance coverage, location, whether or not the professional or organization works with adolescents, and so forth. If possible, present several options and let the family make the decision.

9. Go with the Family on the First Visit

The first visit to a specialist can be a frightening experience for the youth and the parents. After Shanna made several suicidal statements, her mother and I took her to a local hospital for psychiatric evaluation. Shanna was terrified. She held my hand and sat as close to me as she could. Later she let me know how much my presence meant to her.

Shanna's mother was just as frightened as Shanna, and my presence was equally important to her. While Shanna was in the room with us, her mother tried to be strong. But when Shanna went in to be evaluated, her mother shared her own confusion and guilt. She also told me that had I not gone with them, they might not have had the courage to go on their own. She needed someone to be there as much as Shanna did.

Provide Ongoing Support

It is easy to assume that because you have made a referral, your job is done. Actually, your job is just beginning when you make a referral. The young person and the family need your continued support. The sharing group can be an important element in your continued care for the teen. In the group the youth can process the treatment experience and how he or she is handling it. You also need to reach out to the parents. Often they are forgotten. Plan to continue to meet with the parents on a regular basis to process how they are coping with the stress of what has happened. Be aware that there may be additional stress created by the treatment program. Treatment often requires families to participate in painful self-assessment, and the treatment may advocate difficult changes.

REFLECTION QUESTIONS

1. Under what conditions would you make a referral?
2. Make a list of referral agencies in your community to which you could send youth with the following problems:

        drug/alcohol problems   suicidal tendencies
        mental health problems   depression
        physical/mental abuse   in need of assessment

TRAINING TOOLS

1. Visit a local hospital to find out what resources are available there. Find out if the hospital is equipped to make an assessment for each problem that you think might arise in the group. If the hospital cannot make an assessment in a particular area, find out who could make such an assessment.
2. Locate a directory of resources or create one of your own. Brainstorm referral possibilities with other adults and make a list of community resources for each anticipated area of need.

Special Techniques
for Established Groups

From time to time, a special tool may be necessary to help a member of the sharing group work through a problem. The techniques described in this chapter are advanced because they involve more than the basic format outlined in previous chapters. They also are advanced because they require a greater trust level on the part of the group. For this reason, it is recommended that these exercises be used with established and committed groups. These tools do not replace the skills described in previous chapters. The basic function of a sharing group always is to listen and give support. However, the occasion may arise when one of these tools can be used to help a particular member who is struggling with an issue.

A Word of Warning

Many professional counselors would have severe reservations about inexperienced leaders using some of the techniques in this chapter. Assertiveness training, "homework," confrontation, role working conversations, the chair exercise, love/affirmation bombardment, "friend to friend," and walking through a painful experience do not require specialized training. However, anger release, creative fantasy, memory regression, and dreamwork are powerful psychotherapeutic tools which may require the skills of a trained professional. They are included here because they can be helpful tools in the sharing group setting when used by a trained professional or a group leader who has received individualized instruction from a trained professional and is comfortable using the techniques. These four psychotherapeutic tools are not tools for the inexperienced volunteer leader, nor are they tools for youth to use with one another. If a trained professional or skilled leader is not available to the group, these techniques should be reserved for the personal counseling setting so that the group may remain faithful to its primary task: listening.

Before using advanced techniques in the sharing group setting, the group leader would be well advised to inform the parents, perhaps through a letter, that the group has reached an advanced stage and may use special processes to work through the youths' problems and concerns. If the group leader feels that an even stronger form of communication is necessary, depending on the circumstances, he or she could communicate this information through a signed consent form.

Guidelines for Using These Techniques

When using the techniques in this chapter, follow these simple guidelines to ensure that what you do is helpful to the group.

Use Them Sparingly

These tools are not substitutes for listening. Their use should be the exception, not the rule. In the course of a two-hour session, I might use one of these tools if it seemed appropriate. On most weeks I do not use any of them. Listening remains the main tool.

Build up to Them

Never begin with one of these exercises. First allow plenty of time for listening. The need for one of these activities should arise from the sharing. Suggest using an exercise only after carefully listening to the person and clearly determining that the exercise might accomplish something that sharing and listening cannot accomplish.

Use a Technique to Get Through an Impasse

The purpose of the exercises in this chapter is to help a person get through an impasse. They are designed to help an individual start sharing again or to give the person specific help.

Ask the Youth If He or She Is Willing to Try the Exercise

Carefully explain the exercise—what it is, what you are asking them to do, and why you think it might be helpful. Let the members know that there is no guarantee that the exercise will help. Assure them that the exercise may be discontinued at any time if they find it too uncomfortable or overpowering. Then ask the members if they are willing to try the exercise. Do not force or pressure them; they have the final say. I have found that teenagers usually are open to these exercises. It is very important, however, that they have a clear understanding of what they will be doing. Their greatest fear is the unknown.

Access Your Own Comfort Level

Ask yourself if you are comfortable leading the exercise. There is some discomfort in doing anything new. That is to be expected. The issues here are whether or not you have a clear understanding of what you will be doing, why you will be doing it, what you hope to accomplish, and what your feelings of comfort or discomfort are. If you are not comfortable leading the exercise, stick to listening.

Twelve Special Techniques

The following twelve techniques have been used extensively in sharing groups by myself and other group leaders. The techniques usually are helpful in resolving an impasse, and young people respond to them well.

1. Assertiveness Training

> **Problem:** Kim has low self-esteem. She is withdrawn, and she finds it difficult to interact with other youth. She especially finds it difficult to ask for what she needs.
> **Exercise:** Have Kim ask for something from each group member. The group is a safe environment in which she can practice this skill.

Kim did not see anything likable in herself and assumed that everyone else thought the same thing. I asked her to go to each person in the circle—approximately fourteen youth and adults—and ask this question: "What do you like about me?" The ground rule was that a member could share only something that was positive and true—no comments such as "I like your buck teeth" allowed.

After Kim went to each person and received a compliment, I asked her if she believed the person and how it felt to hear the compliment. At the end of the exercise, Kim was beaming. She asked if we could do it again; we did.

On other occasions, I have instructed youth to ask each member for a hug or to practice saying no to requests from the group members. Jimmy could not say no to any request. Anything he was asked to do, he did—whether it was good for him or not. The members spent thirty minutes making requests. Some were made up and some were real. Jimmy's no's became stronger and stronger. The group members began to beg and plead, but his no's had more and more conviction. The group had a lot of fun, and Jimmy began to develop a valuable skill.

The goal of this technique is for persons to practice asserting themselves. Each time that a person asks for something and is rewarded, he or she is reinforcing the notion that it is all right to assert himself or herself.

2. Homework

> **Problem:** Julie needs to continue working on an issue or problem that can be resolved only with a particular person who is not in the group.
>
> **Exercise:** Give Julie a homework assignment. Our young people love to moan and groan when I use the word *homework*. To give a homework assignment means that an individual is to practice a skill or have a conversation with someone outside the group to try to resolve an issue. The person is to report on how things went at the next meeting.

Since her parents' divorce, Julie had become increasingly alienated from her mother. A telephone conversation with her mother the previous month resulted in a total breakdown in communication. In the group Julie talked about how much she wanted to resolve the problems with her mother. The group listened to Julie for quite a while and then indicated several key issues that needed to be addressed. Julie was going to another city for the weekend to visit her mother. Her assignment was to ask her mother to listen to her for ten minutes without making a comment. After this, Julie was to listen to her mother for ten minutes without interrupting. Two of the group members offered to let Julie call them collect just before the conversation with her mother to build her courage.

Having to report to the group the next week put a little healthy pressure on Julie to follow through. The next week a beaming Julie gave her report and thanked the group for helping her to have a conversation that otherwise she never might have had. Julie and her mother still have some issues to resolve, but at least they are talking again.

Adolescents face a lot of issues with parents and peers that cannot be worked through in the group session. The group can give love and support, but the individual must face the situation and do something about it. Giving homework assignments can be extremely helpful.

3. Confrontation

> **Problem:** Something tells you that Rick is not telling the truth or that Rick is not in touch with reality regarding an issue or situation. Or, perhaps you sense that Rick is manipulating the group. You know that letting it slide by without comment would be harmful to Rick and to the group.
>
> **Exercise:** Tell Rick candidly that you do not believe what he is saying and then explain why. One alternative is to have the group do this for you.

Confrontation is a growth factor that you probably will use to some degree in your group. Occasionally, however, you will face a situation that requires something more. You may need to confront a person directly—in a way that goes beyond what you normally would do. Use the third form of confrontation—confronting the individual's self-perception with your perception of him or her.

Something told me that Rick was not telling the truth. He was telling an elaborate story about how he was being victimized by his parents. The story was devoid of any feeling and was full of contradictions. He had been doing this for several weeks. He presented tragedy after tragedy, all of which brought him a lot of attention and sympathy from the group.

As I looked at the group, I could tell that they were bored. My hunch was that Rick was manipulating the group and they knew it. I asked the group if they believed Rick. A dozen people shook their heads no. I then explained to Rick why I was having a hard time believing him. I also shared that I cared about him—not because of the things that he had reported to the group but because of who he was. The group echoed my care for Rick. It was difficult for us to say and it was difficult for Rick to hear, but our expressions of care caused a turning point for Rick. Rick denied that what he had shared was not true, but then he talked about his need for acceptance and love. His dramatic stories ceased.

Confrontation should be used carefully and lovingly, but there are times when avoiding confrontation can be destructive.

4. Role Working Conversations

Problem: Julie needs to have a conversation with someone outside the group, but she is frightened and doesn't know what to say. She needs to rehearse what she will say before she can face her mom.
Exercise: Have Julie practice the conversation with another member of the group.

The group can provide Julie with the opportunity to practice the conversation in several ways. One way is to ask someone to play the role of Julie's mom. Julie tells the volunteer as much as she can about the roles that they will be playing. Then they role play the conversation as it might happen in a face-to-face or phone conversation. Have the two members sit in chairs. If it is to be a telephone conversation, have them sit back to back. If it is to be a face-to-face conversation, have them sit facing each other.

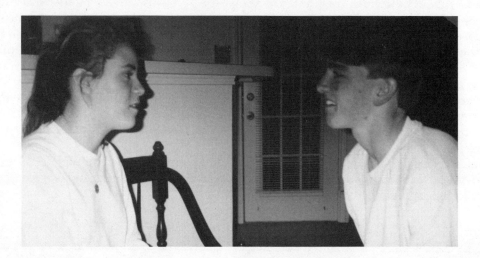

A second approach is to reverse the roles. The group member needing to have the conversation takes the role of the person that he or she is afraid to talk to—a role that he or she probably knows all too well. The volunteer takes the role of the member and models how he or she might handle the conversation. A variation of this second approach is to have several people play the role of the group member so that the member can see several possible alternatives.

Before Julie visited her mother and did her homework assignment, we role worked the conversation for thirty minutes in the group. Julie saw how several other group members would talk to her mother. Julie played the role of her mother and did all the things she was afraid that her mother would do. The other group members responded beautifully. Then Julie switched roles and played herself. The other members, who by then knew a lot about Mom's tactics, played the role of Mom. This helped Julie to build her confidence. Later she said that the actual conversation with her mom was a lot easier than the role working conversations in the group.

5. The Chair Exercise

Problem: A group member needs to have a conversation with someone outside the group.
Exercise: Have the group member role play the conversation by playing both parts.

A modification of role working is the gestalt chair exercise. The problem to be dealt with is the same, but the technique is slightly different. Instead of having someone role play the other person, you leave the second chair empty. The group member visualizes the person that he or she is going to talk to and mentally places this person in the chair. The group member may want to close his or her eyes for a few moments to get a clear mental image of the person. The group member then plays both roles by moving back and forth between the two chairs. From time to time, you may want to ask questions to keep the conversation going—much as a counselor does when working with two people in one session. This exercise is extremely effective and has one important advantage. It enables a person to talk to someone who is physically unavailable, such as a person who has died, who has moved away, or who, for some reason, has become inaccessible.

If Julie had done this exercise, she would have been herself when sitting in one chair and her mother when sitting in the other chair. Julie would have begun by saying what she wanted to say to her mother. When she finished, she would have moved to the other chair to respond in the way that she thought her mother would respond. Then she would have moved back and forth between the two chairs as she played both roles.

Often the group member really doesn't need to talk to the other person. He or she needs to talk to his or her image of that person. Sometimes it's not important what Julie's mom would say; what's important is what Julie *thinks* her mom would say. This is especially true if the other person is inaccessible.

Trudy needed to talk to her father. She needed to express the pain and grief she felt after many years of neglect—years when he had not been a father to her. She used the chair exercise to express her hurt, anger, loneliness, and disappointment. She said things to the chair that she could not bring herself to say to her father's face.

After the exercise, as we were processing the experience, Trudy shared that she knew her father was mentally ill and that he was too fragile to handle all her feelings. She was aware that he probably would never be the father she wanted him to be. She couldn't change him, but talking to him "in the chair" made a world of difference. She said things that she had needed to say for years, and she clarified some things for herself. She left the session feeling more at peace with herself and her father than she had in a long time.

A variation of this exercise is to have the group member put a "part" of himself or herself in the other chair. I asked Troy to visualize his anger and to place it in the chair. He could describe it in great detail. He also could switch chairs with ease and speak for his anger. Troy's anger could say things that Troy would not allow himself to say. His anger could say things that Troy had worked hard to suppress. When Troy was finished, he told us that he had found a friend. He liked his anger. He liked the strong, confident part of himself that his anger expressed. He knew that there were some legitimate reasons for being angry and that his anger was not bad. He simply needed to find healthy ways to channel his anger.

6. Love/Affirmation Bombardment

Problem: Gary is depressed and has a low level of self-worth. He needs to be affirmed so that he can rebuild his self-esteem.

Exercise: Have the group give Gary "Blessings and Bandages."

Sometimes members of the group have low self-esteem. They need a big hug. They need love. They need to know that someone cares, that someone likes them. Our expression of love and concern for them can take a physical form or can be expressed verbally. Sharing groups in our area use an exercise called "Blessings and Bandages." It is a powerful form of love/affirmation bombardment.

Gary lay on the floor face up with his eyes closed. He chose one person to hold his head in his or her lap. The rest of the group formed a circle around Gary and touched him. The members held his hands, arms, legs, and feet. During the exercise, Gary could not say anything. He could only lie on the floor with his eyes closed and listen. One by one, the members affirmed Gary by sharing what they liked and valued about him. There were three ground rules: what was said had to be positive, true, and deeper than a comment written in a school annual—no remarks such as "I think you're a swell person."

It is difficult for most of us to accept a compliment—much less to lie on the floor for a long period of time listening to person after person express warmth and appreciation. But the experience is wonderfully overwhelming. I know of no other exercise that can communicate love and affirmation in the same way.

7. David Stone's "Friend to Friend"

Problem: Lori needs to make a difficult decision. The group has been supportive by listening, but listening is not enough. A decision has to be made.

Exercise: In his book *Friend to Friend: How You Can Help a Friend Through a Problem*, David Stone outlines a process for helping a person make a decision.[1] This method involves asking four questions to guide the person through the process of arriving at his or her own decision. The questions are these:

1) What do you want?
2) What are you feeling?
3) What are you doing to get what you want?
4) What do you need to do?

The first question helps the person to identify what he or she wants to accomplish. The second question helps the person to identify the feelings that are involved. The third question helps the person to get in touch with what he or she is doing—or not doing—to reach the goal. The fourth question identifies what the person needs to do. The process is to ask the four questions again and again. Every time that the person gets stuck and cannot go forward, you go back to the first question: What do you want? This continues until he or she can identify what to do. At that point, he or she has made a decision. The beauty of this approach is that it helps the person to make a decision but forces him or her to reach that decision on his or her own.

The first time I used this process was when Lori confided in our group session that her boyfriend was pressuring her to have sexual intercourse. It would not have been an issue if a part of Lori had not wanted to say yes. Lori was fifteen at the time. We listened to Lori for a long time and then realized that she wanted to make a decision. She was afraid that if she didn't make a definite decision, she probably would wind up saying yes for the wrong reasons.

We used David Stone's approach for about an hour. She clarified her confused feelings and what she wanted. She knew why she wanted to say yes and why she wanted to say no. Finally, she arrived at her decision: she was not ready to make that kind of commitment—and if her boyfriend could not deal with that, then it meant that he was not that concerned about her anyway. Two days later the boyfriend broke up with her and vanished from the scene. His departure reinforced the wisdom of her decision. Lori made the right decision—not because it was what I or the group wanted for her, but because it was her decision.

8. Walking Through a Painful Experience

Problem: Barry is still grieving over his father's death. He misses his father and feels great loss whenever he is reminded of him.

Exercise: Have Barry retell his painful experience among caring friends.

Many young people have had traumatic, painful experiences that still cause them pain. The wound will not heal. Just as a festering wound in the body needs to be lanced and drained, so also a person's pain needs to be lanced and drained by talking about the experience with others. It can be helpful for a person to share the painful experience, to share what happened and what it did to him or her. The youth may have done this before. Everyone in the room already may know all the details. The goal is not to learn anything new. The idea is that narrating the experience will bring back the feelings so that the person can deal with them.

Barry faced the fifth anniversary of his father's death. All day he had been haunted by the memories. Certain images would not go away. By the time he went to the sharing group meeting that evening, he was having a hard time holding himself together. I invited him to retell what had happened the day his father died—what he saw, what he experienced, and what he felt. He had done this at least three times in the past two years in the same group. No one was going to learn anything new.

As Barry retold the story one more time, all the feelings returned. He spent a long time grieving. The pain was still there. His retelling of the story didn't make the pain go away, but it helped a little. Every time Barry cries and tries to come to terms with what has happened in his family, he heals a little bit more.

9. Anger Release Exercise

Problem: Al has a lot of anger but is unable to express it. The unexpressed anger is creating problems. He is afraid that if he expresses his anger, he will hurt others or others will hurt him. Al needs to express his anger in a way that is safe for himself and others.

Exercise: There are many ways that adolescents can express anger: slamming doors, exercising, screaming, pounding a pillow, rolling up a newspaper and pounding the floor until they are exhausted. If some group members cannot bring themselves to do any of these things, consider having them release their anger while the group *gently* restrains them.

Have Al lie on the floor on his back with his arms at his sides. Have the members of the group kneel beside him and gently restrain him by applying pressure. You will need one person to hold each ankle, one to hold each knee, one to hold each hand, and one to hold each shoulder. Al should be gently but securely restrained. The pressure should not be uncomfortable, but Al should be unable to get up. The group should be able to pin him to the floor so that he is unable to hurt himself or anyone else.

Have Al test the restraining power of the group by trying to get up. Once he is convinced that he is pinned, have him think of what makes him angry. He should focus on this as intensely as he can. As he begins to feel the anger, instruct him to throw his anger into his body and try to get up. The first few times he may be timid and hold back, but as he grows to trust the group he will throw everything he is feeling into the struggle to get up. If Al has told you something someone says that makes him angry, you may want to use this to help him.

One young man in our group was infuriated by his dad calling him a wimp. He suggested that I use the term to help him. After he was pinned by the group, I repeatedly told him that he was "a wimp who couldn't even get off the floor." He tried his best to get up, but the group held him. He later told me that it wasn't my voice that he had heard but the voice of his dad. He shared that he was totally exhausted, but that much of his anger had been drained.

This exercise is not for everyone. Some young people simply cannot handle it or "get into it." They cannot put their anger into their struggle to get up. But there are some young people who might be helped by this exercise. These are the young people who need a safe way to express the anger that is churning inside but who cannot bring themselves to let it out in the usual ways.

When working with an angry youth, be sensitive to the depth of the youth's anger and to the potential for harmful effects. Seek the counsel of a professional to determine when a youth has progressed beyond a "healthful" state of anger and refer the youth for counseling.

10. Creative Fantasy

> **Problem:** Rebecca thinks her situation is hopeless. She believes that there is nothing she can do that will change things. She is blind to alternatives and options. She needs to visualize a way that things may be changed to improve her situation.
>
> **Exercise:** Give Rebecca an object and tell her to pretend that it is a magic wand. Tell her that it has the power to change *anything*. Then ask her what she would change in her life.

During a group session, Rebecca expressed her frustration with her family situation. She was miserable and did not see any way that things could get better. I looked around and found a gaudy six-inch plastic knife that some child had left in the room. I handed it to Rebecca and explained that it was a magic wand that could change anything. She became excited and exclaimed, "Oh, yeah! The power of Gray Skull!" After making a few flippant wishes, such as wishing her parents were in a galaxy far, far away, Rebecca began to come up with some excellent ideas. I asked her what was keeping her from doing some of these things. After a long silence, she said, "Me." After that session, the "magic wand" became a regular resource for our group.

All Rebecca needed was to see that she had some alternatives. She needed to see that the only thing keeping her from doing some of these things was herself. She had the answers; she just couldn't see them. By using creative fantasy, she was able to think of alternatives.

11. Memory Regression

> **Problem:** Jolene is still struggling with a painful experience that happened years ago. Sometimes memories can be repressed, or, as is the case with Jolene, an event may have happened so long ago that there are few clear memories of it. It would be difficult for Jolene to retell her experience in the way that Barry retold his experience, but Jolene still needs a way to deal with the pain.
>
> **Exercise:** One way to help Jolene bring back the memories is to have Jolene lie on the floor and close her eyes as you help her to go back in time. Ask Jolene to go back as far as she can remember and to progress in stages, stopping periodically to share a memory and how it felt to be that age. When Jolene comes to the time of the experience, have her share as much as she can remember about what happened and how she felt. Have Jolene relive the experience and process what the event did to her.

Jolene knew that she did not feel loved, but she did not know why. She had a hard time believing that males could care for her. Jolene had felt this way for as long as she could remember. She had told the group that her father had abandoned the family when she was seven, but she did not think that this had anything to do with what she was feeling because it happened so long ago.

To begin the memory regression exercise, we went back as far as Jolene could remember. Her earliest memories were happy ones. Her father was important to her, and they had a special relationship. As we moved forward, things began to change. When her father left, Jolene's world was shattered. She did not understand what had happened or why, but she was sure that it was her fault. Her father did not love her enough to stay, so there must have been something unlovable about her. For several minutes a confused seven-year-old girl in a fifteen-year-old's body lay crying on the floor. As we continued to move forward in time, Jolene related the struggle and pain that her father's absence caused: the financial crises, the pain her mother went through, and all the times she needed her father but he wasn't there. When she finished, she felt a tremendous sense of relief and a sense of being loved by the group which had taken the time to relive that painful time with her.

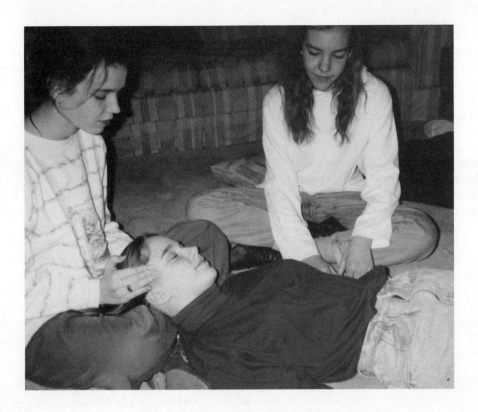

12. Dreamwork

Problem: One of the group members has had a painful, troubling dream. The dream confuses and scares the youth. The dream might be a recurring dream or one of a series of troubling dreams.

Exercise: There are many dream interpretation techniques. One book lists thirty-seven techniques that can be used for spiritual growth.[2] I have found three techniques to be particularly helpful when working with teenagers in the sharing group environment. The key to each approach is to have the young person tell you about the dream and to let him or her interpret the dream with your help.

When using each approach, begin by having the person retell the dream. Ask the youth to share as much detail as possible. What is the first thing that he or she remembers in the dream? What happened? Who was in the dream? Did he or she recognize anyone? It is particularly important to ask how he or she felt at each stage of the dream. How the dream ended and how the youth felt at the end of the dream are also important. Keep asking questions until you are sure that you know everything the person can remember about the dream.

If the dream has recurred with variations or if there has been a series of dreams, have the member retell the other dreams in the same way. Look for patterns and similarities. When the youth has finished, use one or more of the following approaches to help him or her make sense of the dream.

Self Interpretation. Before trying any other approach, try to let the group member interpret the dream. What does he or she think the dream means? What is the dream's "message"? The best interpreter of the dream is the one who has dreamed it. Even when others offer an interpretation, the dreamer knows if it sounds right or not. After you have helped an adolescent retell a dream and remember the details and feelings, the adolescent often knows what the message is. However, if the youth cannot make sense of the dream alone, offer one or both of the following options.

Correlation. This approach helps the person look for similarities between the dream and what is going on in his or her life. Are any of the characters in the dream real people, or do the characters resemble real people in any way? Are there similarities between events, situations, or feelings in the dream and those in the person's life? Could the dream be a symbolic rehashing of something the person is going through right now?

Jack had a series of terrifying nightmares. Each dream was different, yet all had striking similarities. In each dream, Jack's father was trying to kill him, and Jack was hiding, terrified. Jack's parents had separated about two weeks before the dreams started.

At first, Jack could not see a pattern in the dreams. They made no sense to him. I suggested one possibility was that the dreams could be telling him how he felt about what was going on in his life. We began to look for points of contact between the dreams and the situation at home. It did not take Jack very long to find many similarities and to figure out what the dreams meant. His parents' separation had caused a lot of anger and hostility, particularly on the part of his father. Jack felt that his father's anger was directed at him, and he was terrified. In his dreams he physically hid from his father. In his life he was hiding emotionally.

Gestalt. The gestalt approach to dreamwork assumes that every character in the dream, whether human or not, is a part of the dreamer. This approach is particularly helpful with dreams that are highly symbolic and do not seem to make any sense.

If we used the gestalt approach to interpret Jack's dream, we would consider both the character of the father and the character of Jack to be parts of Jack. This would suggest that a part of Jack is angry and hostile and wants to lash out, while another part of Jack is frightened by these feelings and wants to hide from them. Knowing Jack and how much he has repressed his anger, I am inclined to think that this interpretation explains a lot about Jack.

The important thing to remember when using each approach is not to impose your own interpretations but to offer several options and see if any of these helps the person understand what is going on in his or her life. If a person suddenly becomes excited and has an "ah-ha!" reaction, then the interpretation has hit close to home.

Dreamwork with teenagers is important for two reasons. First, there are times when we can help teenagers to make sense of a dream and "read" its message. Dreams are a way that the unconscious can send us important messages about things going on in our lives. Recurring dreams may be caused by our inability to read the message. If we can help to shed some light on the message, then the youth can begin to come to terms with the message and do something about it.

A second reason that dreamwork is important to young people is that it helps them to process a dream—whether or not they understand it. At times dreams can be vivid and terrifying. By processing a dream, a youth realizes that dreams are normal. I have known youth who thought that they were sick or going crazy just because they had a highly symbolic dream that unnerved them. Letting youth know that most of us have these dreams and that dreams are nothing to be frightened of can be very reassuring.

* * *

All of the techniques described in this chapter have been used with young people in sharing groups. All have been helpful at times, and all have failed on occasion. The key is always to offer the approach to the young person with the hope that it might help. The group members are the ones who must decide if they want to try any of these approaches, just as they are the ones who must decide which interpretations fit.

REFLECTION QUESTIONS

1. Review the "problems" mentioned in this chapter. What problems might arise in your group?
2. Which exercises in this chapter would you be comfortable using? Which ones would you avoid?
3. Are there other exercises that you would add to those described in this chapter?

TRAINING TOOLS

1. Have the members of your leadership team practice role working for two or three issues. Choose real issues that individuals in the group need to address in conversations with others. Then have each person work through the conversation with a volunteer from the group.
2. Try the chair exercise. You may want to practice the exercise using both forms: one person playing both roles, and one person talking to a part of himself or herself (anger, shyness, etc.).
3. Divide into dyads and use David Stone's "Friend to Friend" approach to practice helping someone make a decision. Use ten minutes for the process and then change roles and do it again. Be sure to debrief after the experience. Your reactions will tell you a lot about how the sharing group members might react to this exercise.
4. Practice dreamwork. Have two or three people share one of their dreams with the group. As each person shares, use the approaches suggested in this chapter to help the person make sense of the dream.

10

Dealing with
Special Problems

Over the years, all of the things mentioned in this chapter have happened in groups that I have led. After talking to other sharing group leaders, I have discovered that sooner or later these things will happen to most of us. If we know what things are likely to happen and how others have handled them, then we are better prepared to deal with them when they arise.

No One Has Anything to Share

I consider myself to be a good group leader. I know the young people in our group. I know what's going on in their lives. I know how to "draw them out" and get them to share. Even so, four or five times a year I draw a blank. Zero. Nothing. The group members don't have anything they want to share. Through trial and error, I have learned to respect this and to work with it rather than against it.

The one guideline that I can give you is this: if no one has anything to share, then close the sharing group session. Have the closing prayer and make a clear break before moving into informal conversation or other activities. It is important for the group to understand that the sharing group time is for sharing, not visiting. When we first offered sharing groups at our church, I did not make this distinction to the group. The result was that some of the group members came to the group expecting to "visit."

Parents' Fears and Misconceptions

Occasionally parents become concerned and fearful about what is going on in a sharing group. A group member may make the confidentiality policy sound like the group is being secretive, such as the girl who "dared" her mother to try to find out what was going on in the group. The mother took the dare and phoned me! Parents may hear part of a conversation on the phone and let their imaginations fill in the blanks. Or, a youth may share his or her somewhat distorted view of what a sharing group is about, as was the case with the group member who told the church board that "we gripe about our parents."

This is a legitimate concern that needs to be treated with respect. Parents do not know what is being said in the group, and they are aware that teens will be dealing with family frustrations and sensitive issues involving them. There are several things we can do to minimize this problem.

Make Sure that Parents Understand What a Sharing Group Is

If you clearly communicate the sharing group model with the parents before you begin the group and if you have a good relationship with the parents, the problem will be minimal. Also remember to inform parents of the various techniques used in group sessions so that fears or misconceptions may be alleviated. As suggested in chapter 9, it is advisable to seek the support of parents before using more advanced techniques. Although such measures will help to minimize misunderstandings, some problems are simply unavoidable.

Keep an Open Line of Communication with Parents

I once received a phone call from an angry parent who complained that the sharing group kept her junior high daughter in session until 10:30 P.M. I knew that the group was over at 9:00 P.M. After we checked our stories, we discovered that her daughter had told her the group lasted until 10:30 so that she could be with her boyfriend.

Clear communication with parents is crucial. There is no way to anticipate all the problems that might arise. The important thing is that parents know they can contact you to clear up any confusion or misinformation.

When a Problem Arises, Act Quickly

When a problem arises, act quickly by directly addressing the problem. I cannot break confidentiality, but I can deal with parents' fears and misconceptions. If the problem involves a sharing group that I do not work with personally, I know that I can contact the group leader to get the correct information. I always keep in mind that my role is an extension of the parents' role and that I cannot minister to their children without their support and trust. If I let something slide—if I do not act quickly—then I can lose their trust.

When to Close and Reopen a Group

Several groups in our area are now in their fifth year of existence. People have come and gone. Some members have graduated from high school, have become involved in other sharing groups, or simply have stopped coming. New members have taken their places. New seventh graders have come into the program. New families have joined the church. Group members have brought their friends. Young people who were not interested one year have become interested the next year. If you are to have an ongoing group, one that is a regular part of your youth program, then you have to decide when to close and reopen a group.

I have found it best to close a group after two or three sessions. By then a group usually has bonded and has built their trust level to the point where they can share sensitive issues. After this point, having people come in and out of the group is disruptive. When a group is closed, it is understood that those who are in the group have made a commitment to continued regular attendance and that the group will not take in any new members until the next time the group is reopened.

Occasionally a group will bond the first session. Something is shared that is so significant to the life of the group that a deep level of trust is built. Bringing in a new person the second week would inhibit further sharing. If the group bonds the first session, then close the group.

Groups also need a time to end, a time when members can be released from their commitment and when new members can come into the group. Our groups have found it best to end and reform three times a year. We open groups in the fall, spring, and summer. The fall groups form about a week after school starts and run through mid-December. It is very difficult to continue the groups during finals and the holiday season. Some groups may vote to continue during this period, but most are eager to take a break. Spring groups reform after the Christmas break in January and continue until mid-May. These groups end before finals, giving members approximately a two-week break before the summer groups begin. Summer groups form as soon as school is out and end when school begins in the fall. Summer groups tend to pick up a lot of youth who do not participate during the academic year due to school pressures. Often parents do not allow their children to participate during the school year but allow them to become involved during the summer months.

Whenever you reopen a group, publicize the reopening for two or three weeks before the first session. Circulate or post sign-up sheets and contact anyone whom you feel might benefit from the group—new teenagers, adolescents going through crises, and so forth. Allow those young persons who want to continue participating in the group to do so. They will provide continuity and leadership.

A Break in Confidentiality

Our groups have had a major break in confidentiality only twice in nine years, but both times it "killed" the group. A break in confidentiality is one of the worst things that can happen in a group. The most effective time to deal with this problem is before it happens. The importance of confidentiality cannot be overemphasized to the group. Once a confidence has been broken, there is very little that you can do. The young people need to understand that the first time they tell one person a confidential tidbit, they probably have destroyed the group for themselves and everyone else.

When a confidentiality has been broken, immediately confront the problem head on. Do this in the group with the person who broke confidentiality present. Let the group process their feelings. Be firm but redemptive. Confidentiality usually is not broken because of viciousness or a desire to hurt anyone. Usually, a group member simply cannot resist telling one person something that was said in the group. The person who breaks confidentiality is more important than the act; even so, the act profoundly affects the group and everyone in it.

The first time that one of our groups experienced a break in confidentiality, a group member confronted the "guilty" person in the next session. It was an extremely painful experience for everyone. We thought that we had resolved the situation by the end of the session, but within three weeks the group disbanded. The youth did not hold a grudge, but the trust level in the group simply was not there anymore.

On another occasion, a member of the group privately shared with me that a confidence had been broken, but she was unwilling to share the information with the group. Since I did not know firsthand that a confidence had been broken—I had only a report of a break—I did not feel that I could confront the person. One by one the other group members found out about the break, and the group's trust level slowly died. A month later we voted to end the group.

If young people cannot be absolutely sure that what they say is confidential, then they will not share. Our youth are very vocal about this. If this expectation is made clear at the beginning and if the young people come to value the group, then the group should not have many problems. Our current group is now in its third year without a break in confidentiality.

Conflict Within the Group

Andrea and Terri had been in our group for two years when their friendship ended. The effect on the group was dramatic. Everyone in the group knew what was going on, but little was said. A few times Terri would bring up a veiled concern about an unnamed friend, and Andrea would look at the floor. A sharing group can be an extremely helpful environment in which to work through such a conflict. The entire group can benefit by seeing two people work through a conflict rather than allow it to end the relationship.

If you attempt to deal with a conflict between two group members in a group session, both need to give their consent. They also need to speak in "I statements" about their own experiences and feelings. Anything that even remotely resembles a "you statement" or an attack should be avoided. Begin by having both members express what is positive in their relationship; then have them share what is bothering them. Remind both members to use their listening skills and to try to understand what the other is saying. One technique is to have each person repeat what he or she heard the other person say—to the other person's satisfaction—before responding. If Andrea says that she is angry at Terri because Terri no longer calls her or spends time with her, then Terri needs to repeat to Andrea what Andrea has just said. When she has done this to Andrea's satisfaction, Terri can respond. This ensures that each is hearing the other correctly and that the communication is flowing smoothly. This also makes dealing with conflict a lot easier! If either person does not give his or her consent to work on the problem in the group, *do not proceed*. I learned this the hard way.

Susan and Shannon were in the same group. After a break in their friendship, Susan wanted to deal with the hurt and rejection that she felt. Shannon did not say no, but she was withdrawn. The group decided that it was all right for Susan to deal with her feelings as long as she dealt with herself only and did not say anything about Shannon. Susan was a mature, sensitive girl who processed her feelings in a way that seemed healthy. She never attacked Shannon but dealt honestly with the hurt she felt. Several times she tried to get a response from Shannon, but she had no success.

Although Shannon never gave her consent, she also never objected. She sat in silence, even though everything Susan shared concerned Shannon. The next week Shannon failed to show up at the sharing group. Within a couple of months she had dropped out of the youth group and the church. Shannon never did say anything, but it is probable that she perceived the session to be an attack by Susan supported by the group. Shannon finally shared her reaction—she shared it through her absence.

Manipulative Behavior

Youth who share get a lot of attention from the group. Occasionally a young person may try to get attention from the group in unhealthy ways. A person may fabricate things to share, dominate the group with his or her overwhelming needs, or try to use the sharing group to force another person into a relationship with him or her. If group members need attention, then we need to give it to them; however, we also need to limit the amount of time and attention that any one member receives. Sometimes we may choose to give an entire session to one person. But if we do this week after week, then we hurt the group as a whole. The group does not exist to meet the needs of only one member, or only a few members.

If a person is dominating the group, remind him or her that there are others in the group who also need time. If this is unacceptable to the person or if the dominating behavior continues, a referral may be necessary so that the person can get help for some needs in another setting. If you have to confront someone whose behavior is unacceptable, let the person know that it is the behavior, not the person, that is unacceptable.

Anxiety Attack or Hyperventilation

Rarely does a group member have an anxiety attack, but when it does happen it can be very frightening. A young person's emotions can become so "out of control" that he or she has an anxiety attack. The youth is terrified but does not know why. Perhaps the youth is experiencing an emotion or facing a situation that terrifies him or her. He or she may begin to breathe rapidly and hyperventilate. The increased oxygen in the blood can produce physical symptoms.

If a group member has an anxiety attack, have the person lie down and try to relax. Assure the person that he or she is all right and tell the person to slow his or her breathing. You may want to have the individual breathe with a paper sack over his or her face to increase the carbon dioxide level in the blood. After you have reassured the individual, explain what is happening. Get the person "into his or her head" and "out of his or her feelings" by talking about something else. Avoid "feeling language" and the topic that precipitated the attack. If the attack is isolated, then follow-up measures probably are not necessary. However, if the attack is repeated, you may need to refer the individual to a professional who can assess the problem.

Keeping the Group from Becoming a Clique

A sharing group is a clique by its very nature—at least in the positive sense of the term. As young people share, they bond with one another and develop a closeness among them. They share experiences that others do not share. They want to be together. They may be more comfortable with one another than with those outside the group. Much of this is positive. In the New Testament, this closeness is called *koinonia*, the fellowship of the Holy Spirit. On the other hand, cliques can become exclusive. The youth group can become divided into "us" and "them." This is why it is important to understand that friends and cliques are two sides of the same thing. *My friends* are friends. *You and your friends* constitute a clique. If you sense that your sharing group is becoming exclusive and thus is creating problems, there are some things that you can do.

Periodically Open the Group to New Members

The best way to minimize the risk of the sharing group becoming a clique is to make sure that the group is not limited to a set group of people. Allow the membership of the group to change from time to time. You can accomplish this by reopening the group at regular intervals to anyone who wants to participate.

Make Sure that Group Members Interact with Non-Members in Other Settings

Another way to prevent the sharing group from becoming a clique is to involve the sharing group members with the rest of the youth group in other settings. Several of our groups wanted to hold sharing group sessions on trips. They wanted only those who were in the sharing group at home to meet in the sharing group on the trip. This would have meant that a small group would have retreated from the main group. We handled the situation by affirming that we can have sharing group sessions on trips and retreats only if everyone on the trip is included. During the past several years, we have built evening sharing group sessions into the design of all trips and retreats. This allows the young people to share the significant events of the day and to deal with any problems that may have developed. *No one is excluded.*

When a Group Begins to Die

Bret and Corie, the adults who led one of our sharing groups, decided to let their group die. At one time, their group had been the largest and most committed group in our church. Week after week the members dealt with important issues. The group was a vital part of the young persons' lives. Then, things slowly began to change. Some of the young people who had had strong needs received the help that they needed, and they no longer were motivated to come. Things outside the group were of more interest to them. Three of the most active members graduated from high school and went off to college. A couple of youth dropped out after having a personality conflict. Suddenly, there were not enough young people to make the group work. Even the few remaining faithful members were discouraged. When attempts to recruit new members and build the group failed, they decided to let the group die. This gave the adult leaders a chance to take a break, and it gave the remaining members a chance to join other groups.

Several techniques may help to salvage a group that is in trouble. The best approach is to confront the problem head on. First, share your perception of the problem and then invite the group members to share their perceptions and feelings. Allow plenty of time for "ventilation." Expand the meeting time to allow a complete "airing" of feelings and thoughts. Some groups use an all-night slumber party format for this purpose.

Once this has been done, have the group remember what was good about the group. Challenge the group members to recovenant to the group. Some groups make friendship bracelets to symbolize the commitment that the group members are making to one another. No group should be allowed to die unless everything possible has been done to salvage the group. When a sharing group dies, the causes for the group's death can seep into the youths' other relationships.

Sometimes it is best to let a group die. Like everything else, a group has a natural life-span. A group can run its course. There can be a loss of interest, commitment, and attendance. If the number of regular participants drops below six to eight, a group can lose its ability to sustain itself. This can happen for a variety of reasons: a break in confidentiality, a conflict in the group, a loss of graduating members, a loss of youth whose needs have been met, and so forth.

When a group ends, use the last session to bring closure to the group experience. The young people can remember what was good about the group and what they have shared. They can express affection and gratitude. They also can express the sorrow they may feel because the group is ending. A closing session is a healing experience for the youth and sets the stage for the youths' participation in another group at another time.

You may want to use "Blessings and Bandages" (see chapter 9) for a closing exercise. We use this exercise to close the small-group experience at summer camps in our area. Each member writes in a notebook what he or she appreciates about each person; then each member says what he or she thinks and feels to each person. With a group of eight to ten people who know one another well, this can take several hours. Other good ideas for giving the group closure can be found in the *Group* magazine article "When To Let A Group Die."[1]

REFLECTION QUESTIONS

1. Which of the potential problems mentioned in this chapter might your group encounter? How would you deal with each?
2. What problems not mentioned in this chapter might a group in your church face?

TRAINING TOOLS

1. Introduce the sharing group model at a parents' meeting. Discuss with the parents their concerns and fears. How will you maintain good communication with the parents?
2. Present the sharing group model to your church board or council. What are their concerns?

Training Teenagers
to Lead Groups

I was leaving town for two weeks and was concerned about our sharing group. Several of the members were going through significant personal struggles and depended on the group for support. The group had an adult co-leader, but he had been with the group for only three weeks. He loved the young people and the young people loved him, but he did not know how to run a group—and he told me so.

Although I was concerned about the group and about individual members, I was not worried because I knew that the group could run itself. The group had been together for over a year; they knew what to do. Several of the youth were capable of running the group and had done so on occasion. I trusted the group. In particular, I trusted Rebecca. Rebecca, a junior in high school, was a natural group leader. She was trusted and respected by the group. She was the one whom the group wanted to lead the session while I was gone. When I returned two weeks later, I learned that my trust had been well placed. The group had continued in my absence almost as if I had been there.

I never cease to be amazed by what young people can do. At summer camp, youth play an important role in leading our groups. On three occasions, groups at camp have been led solely by youth when the adult leaders had to leave in the middle of the week because of emergencies. One of the high schools in our area asked young people from our sharing group to set up and run a school program in which youth could talk about their problems. Even junior high youth are capable of providing significant leadership.

Youth can be leaders in sharing groups. There is no reason to exclude them from this role. However, sharing and relinquishing leadership to young people must be done with care. Youth need to be prepared for leadership.

The Role of Adults

Our church has a policy that no group can meet without the presence of at least one adult. I am in complete agreement with this policy. Adults are needed in sharing groups. They have a crucial role to play. Developing youth as sharing group leaders does not mean that our goal is to eliminate adult participation. Certain things that adults bring to the group are essential.

Young People Need Adults

Young people need adults. They need the maturity and wisdom that adults offer. They need the wealth of life experiences and perspectives that adults have. They need the love and support that come from caring adults. One of the main reasons that youth sign up for a sharing group is the adult leader. They sign up because they trust that adult. They care about that adult, and they know that adult cares about them. Youth also need adults to set boundaries, to make the group safe, and to role model how the group is to interact.

Young People Want Adults

The young people I work with want an adult in the group. They do not trust their peers to do everything. They are aware that the adult plays a significant role in the group, and they are aware that they need that adult. They need the relationship with that adult—the love, the care, and the support that the adult can bring to the group.

Shared Leadership

What I am suggesting is shared leadership. Both adults and youth have something to contribute. Sometimes the adult will take a stronger role; other times the adult will step back to let youth lead.

Kim was leading the group as they worked with Andrea. I was present, but Kim was leading because she knew Andrea better than I did. Kim had talked to Andrea during the week and knew what was going on. For thirty minutes, Kim led the group as Andrea shared her home problems, her depression, and her fear. I was amazed; I could not have done a better job myself. Then Kim and Andrea got "stuck." The sharing stopped, and neither of them knew what to do. Kim gave me a look that said "help." I remembered something that Andrea had said earlier to Kim, and I asked Andrea a question. Andrea resumed her sharing, and Kim resumed the role of leader.

In another session, Jamie was relating her feelings about being sexually abused. I knew that Linda had been working on the same issue in therapy, so I turned to Linda and asked her to share with Jamie. For the next thirty minutes, my role shifted to that of listener while Linda shared with Jamie.

Often another member of the group is better equipped to deal with a given issue or situation than I am. Sometimes I am not aware of a member's ability to help; but, if I will step back, that person will come forward on his or her own.

The Training Process

Any youth can function as the leader of a session dealing with a particular person or situation. This requires little training. However, if we want young people to assume the role of co-leader or to lead the group on a regular basis, then we need to be more intentional in preparing them. I have found the following process to be helpful.

1. Encourage Youth to Participate in the Group

Young people learn how a sharing group works by participating in the life of the group. They learn by sharing and interacting with others as they share. After youth participate in the group for a period of time, what the group does becomes second nature to them. Participation is the first step to becoming a leader.

2. Move to Shared Leadership

Early in the life of the group, the adult probably will function as the main leader and will serve as a leadership skills role model. As the youth become familiar with what is going on in the group, they will interact with one another more and more. When this happens, leadership is shared. No one says, "Jim, will you assume leadership of the group and work with Kerry?" It just happens.

3. Identify Youth with Leadership Abilities

As the group continues to mature, youth with natural leadership abilities will emerge. Some members are good listeners; they know what questions to ask when. When these youth are helping a person share, the sharing group process works. At this stage, the adult can step back even farther and defer to these youth. If I can be of help to Bill but know that Kevin can do almost as well, then I should let Kevin help Bill. I can step in to assist if necessary, but experience has taught me that I rarely need to step in when Kevin helps someone.

4. Give Specific Youth Opportunities to Lead

I have found it helpful to provide opportunities for specific youth to lead the group. When a youth wants to claim time in the group, I may ask another member to provide the leadership. Or, if I have to leave the room or miss a session, I may ask a youth to take my place. Allowing a youth to become the leader for a short duration is extremely helpful, especially when he or she knows that I will not be there to step in.

5. Allow Youth to Be Co-Leaders and Leaders

Most churches have youth who are capable of leading a group on their own if they are properly trained and are given the opportunity. There is no reason that an experienced group member with leadership skills cannot serve as co-leader with an adult leader. During her junior and senior years in high school, Rebecca was my co-leader. The group knew Rebecca's abilities, and they were comfortable with her in that role. No one expected her to be me or to have the same skills that I have. She was a youth, not an adult. But she was a co-leader, and she did the job well.

There also is no reason that youth cannot lead groups on their own under special circumstances. A mature senior high can run a junior high group effectively. Our groups have done this at camps and retreats.

6. Instruct Youth in Helping Skills

The youth receive most of their training for helping others to deal with problems through informal participation in the life of the sharing group. However, there are ways that we can give youth "formal training" in helping skills. I recommend the training model created by Barbara Varenhorst, which is presented in her book *Training Teenagers For Peer Ministry* (Group, 1988). Barbara has been training teenagers to use basic counseling skills for over twenty years. Her book contains a comprehensive training program to teach young people skills such as are needed in a sharing group. Most of the youth in our sharing groups have been through Barbara's program, and the experience has made a dramatic difference in their abilities. During the training programs, I have been able to identify several of our young people who are natural helpers. The sharing group then becomes a lab in which the youth can use the skills that they have been taught. When it is time to help someone, they know what to do.

Teenagers are capable of being competent group leaders, if given the chance. If we take time to train them and to give them opportunities to use their skills, then youth can play a profound leadership role in any sharing group.

REFLECTION QUESTIONS

1. What is your philosophy of youth leadership?
2. Would you be comfortable sharing leadership with a youth in a group?
3. Who are the natural leaders in your group? What abilities or skills do they have? What skills do they need to be taught?
4. Would you consider allowing a youth to lead a group on his or her own? If so, under what conditions?

TRAINING TOOLS

1. As a group, discuss your philosophy of youth leadership. What concerns have been raised? How would you address these concerns?
2. Have the group brainstorm what having a youth as a co-leader could add to the group. Then discuss how this could benefit the youth who is leading the group.
3. Compare the results of this discussion with your philosophy of youth ministry.

Conclusion

Whether you are working with a sharing group or are thinking about beginning one, I invite you to trust.

Trust the process. It works. It has worked for a lot of people in a variety of churches and settings. The sharing group process is built on sound principles that have been used successfully for a long time.

Trust your group members. The youth who comprise your group are no different from the youth who comprise already existing groups. Young people are young people. They need what a sharing group can offer, and, given half a chance, they will make the group work.

Trust yourself. If you love youth and have a good relationship with them, then you are halfway there. You can learn the rest. Like those of us who already are involved in sharing groups, somehow you will muddle through and will find yourself involved in a profound ministry.

Trust God. Trust that God is at work in your ministry and in the young people's lives. Trust that God can use your love and efforts to help group members become whole. Whenever we reach out to touch the life of another human being, we are not alone. This is what makes ministry possible.

Also, remember that nothing is perfect. There will be problems. The sharing group model presented in this book works, but it has limitations. I have tried to make you aware of as many of these limitations as possible, but new problems continuously arise. Each of us must deal with new situations to the best of our abilities. Adapt this model to fit your needs. Use love and sensitivity to adjust it to your situation and your young people's needs so that you can make a difference in their lives.

Notes

1. Bearing One Another's Burdens

1. Howard Clinebell, *The Mental Health Ministry of the Local Church* (Abingdon Press, 1972) p. 161.
2. *Ibid.*, p. 164.
3. *Ibid.*, p. 169.
4. *Ibid.*, pp. 169-70.
5. "Today's Adolescents Dealing with Different Choices and Great Risks," *Chicago Tribune*, 7 December 1986.
6. "Kids Coping Techniques," *Group Magazine*, February 1987, p. 13.
7. David Stone, *Spiritual Growth in Youth Ministry* (Group Books, 1986), pp. 156–70.

2. Biblical and Theological Foundations

1. See *Childhood and Society* by Erik Erickson for information about how life experiences shape our ability to trust, and see *Stages in Faith* by James Fowler for information about how this connects with our ability to trust God.

3. Putting Your Group Together

1. To avoid misunderstanding and misconceptions, it is helpful to inform parents of the various techniques used in the sharing group. Before using the advanced techniques described in chapter 9, the group leader may want to seek the support of the parents.

5. Eight Factors in Personal Growth

1. Robert Carkhuff, *Helping and Human Relations: A Primer for Lay and Professional Helpers* (Holt, Rinehart, & Winston, 1969), pp. 36–39.
2. Duane Ewers, *Do You Care? Compassion in the Sunday School* (Discipleship Resources, 1988).

6. Twelve Covenant Guidelines for Sharing Groups

1. Barbara Varenhorst, *Training Teenagers for Peer Ministry* (Group Books, 1988), pp. 72–75.
2. David Stone, *Friend to Friend: How You Can Help a Friend Through a Problem* (Group Books, 1983).
3. It is wise to ensure that parents are aware of the various techniques being used in the sharing group. Although what is shared within the group is confidential, parents do have the right to know the kinds of exercises and techniques in which their children will be participating. Before using the more advanced techniques described in chapter 9, the group leader may want to inform parents that the group has reached an advanced stage and will be using special techniques as they listen to one another's problems and concerns.
4. For more information, read "Child Abuse Reporting Requirements: Liabilities and Immunities for Clergy," *The Journal of Pastoral Care and Counseling*, vol. 44, no. 3 (1990), pp. 244–48.
5. There may be times when breaking a confidentiality becomes an ethical or legal consideration. The group leader will find helpful guidance related to such issues in John C. Bush and William Harold Tiemann's *The Right to Silence* (Abingdon Press, 1989). Bush and Tiemann make this statement regarding the right to privilege in counseling groups:

> Everything said in such [sharing] groups could very well become available testimony in court. Is that scary? It certainly should be. It is the single most dangerous threat to the practice of CPE today. But what if the patient or client signs a waiver granting permission for confidential material to be revealed in the group process? Does this common practice provide protection? Not likely. In fact, the opposite seems more probable. The existence of such a signed document may constitute evidence that the patient waived all claim to privilege by consenting to a revelation of the conversation. Thus, every aspect of the relationship becomes open to the courts (p. 167).

Other helpful information regarding legal and ethical issues as they pertain to sharing groups can be found in chapters 11, 14, 15, and 16.

7. Twelve Tools for Sharing Groups

1. Keith Olson, *Counseling Teenagers* (Group Books, 1984), pp. 165–201.

8. Making Referrals

1. Keith Olson, *Counseling Teenagers* (Group Books, 1984), p. 235.
2. For more information regarding child abuse reporting requirements, see "Child Abuse Reporting Requirements: Liabilities and Immunities for Clergy," *The Journal of Pastoral Care and Counseling*, vol. 44, no. 3 (1990), pp. 244–48.

9. Special Techniques for Established Groups

1. David Stone, *Friend to Friend: How You Can Help a Friend Through a Problem* (Group Books, 1983), pp. 18–19.
2. Louis M. Savary et al., *Dreams And Spiritual Growth: A Christian Approach to Dreamwork* (Paulist Press, 1984).

10. Dealing with Special Problems

1. Joani Schultz, "When to Let a Group Die," *Group Magazine*, March/April 1986, pp. 8–11.

Appendix A

Survey of Youth's Needs

Name: _____ Phone: _____

Address: _____

_____

Age: _____ Grade: _____

Family Background

Deaths in Family

Who: _____

When: _____

Divorce or Separation of Parents: _____
                                          (when)

Second Marriages

Mother: _____
                    (when)

Father: _____
                    (when)

Major Illnesses in Family: _____

Major Changes in Family: _____
                                   (Moves, Job Changes, etc.)

Other Crises in Family

_____

_____

_____

Personal Situation

My needs/concerns:

_____ loneliness _____ anger _____ school problems

_____ depression _____ conflict _____ peer problems

_____ suicidal _____ health _____ family problems

_____ other: _____

Three words I would use to describe myself:

_____   _____   _____

If I could change anything about my family, it would be

_____ .

If I could change anything about myself, it would be

_____ .

If I could change anything about my peer relationships, it would be

_____ .

What I Want from a Sharing Group

_____ a place to talk about my concerns

_____ people who will listen

_____ people I can get close to

_____ a place where I can help others

Group Preference Profile

Type of Group:

_____ sharing (talking about concerns and struggles)

_____ prayer and share (sharing and spiritual growth)

_____ spiritual growth (focus on our relationship with God and faith struggles)

_____ special needs (death, divorce, graduation, etc.)

_____ other: _____

Members of Group:

_____ junior highs only

_____ senior highs only

_____ both junior and senior highs

Frequency of Meetings:

_____ weekly _____ bi-weekly _____ monthly _____ on retreats

day: _____ time: _____ duration: 1 hr._____

90 min._____

2 hr._____

place: _____ church _____ home

Additional Information

Someone in our church who would benefit from a sharing group:

Name: _____ Phone: _____

Address: _____

_____

Reason: _____

Someone outside our church who would benefit from a sharing group:

Name: _____ Phone: _____

Address: _____

_____

Reason: _____

Appendix B

Sharing Group Guidelines

Purpose

A sharing group is a group of people who agree to meet regularly to support one another through problems and struggles. They do this by sharing, listening, and following a few basic guidelines that make the group safe and helpful.

Guidelines

Attend Regularly

Attend the group as often as possible. Make it a priority. Being together on a regular basis helps to build trust and to bring us closer together. Dropping in and out, arriving late, or leaving early is disruptive.

Share

Share your feelings, concerns, and problems, and interact with others when they are sharing. This does not mean that you must have a "problem" each week or that you should talk frequently in the group. It means that you are to be involved—to be an active and vital member of the group. The purpose of the sharing group is not to eavesdrop on others as they share or to pick up juicy bits of gossip. Rather, by sharing our feelings, thoughts, and concerns, we become closer to others and feel that we belong to the group. We get out of the group only as much as we put into the group. There are no observers in a sharing group; there are only participants. If you come, come prepared to share.

Focus on the Person Who Is Sharing

Our time together is limited and valuable. It is to be used for sharing and giving support. When someone is sharing, he or she has the floor—and our attention—until he or she is through sharing. Do not visit, chatter, or have side conversations. Save these things for later—after the group meeting. When a person is sharing, focus your attention on the person and what he or she is saying. Daydreaming, leaving the room, or having side conversations may be interpreted as disregard for the person who is sharing. If you want to share something from your life, such as a similar experience, then share only what is helpful to the person you are trying to help. Do not "steal the show" by shifting the focus to yourself. When someone is sharing, the floor is his or hers. Our task is to focus on the individual and to help if we can.

The Person Is More Important than the Story

The important thing in a sharing group is the people—their experiences, their feelings, and what's going on in their lives. Sometimes we may be tempted to become absorbed in "the story"—what happened there and then. By focusing on the here and now—how a person feels about what happened and how he or she is dealing with those feelings—we keep the focus on the person. We need to know what this event or relationship is doing to the person and what he or she is feeling. Sometimes people hide behind a story to keep from dealing with their feelings. By refusing to be drawn into the story, we are able to help people deal with their feelings and their struggles.

Our Task Is to Understand the Problem, Not to Solve It

The key to helping someone with a problem is listening—trying to understand what the person is experiencing and how it affects him or her. We may be tempted to try to solve the problem quickly by putting a band-aid on it. But it is the individual's solution, not our solution, that is important. Often being heard and cared for *is* the solution. Many times there literally is nothing that we can do except to care. We can't change what is going on at someone's home or at his or her school, but we can change what is going on in the group right now. We can care and let the person know that we care. After we have done this, we can give the person alternatives—if the person wants them. What the person does is still his or her choice.

Allow Time for Silence

A person can answer only one question at a time. If we ask a person to consider something, then we need to give that person time to think and to respond. The person also may need time to allow feelings to come to the surface. Bombarding someone with questions or comments is not helpful. If we raise our hand to ask a question before a person has finished talking, we may disrupt what is taking place. The moment that our hand goes up, we stop listening and become focused on what *we* want to say. It is better to wait until the person has finished talking to see if our question or comment is still appropriate. Remember, the focus always should be on the person who is sharing—on his or her concerns and needs rather than our curiosity.

Use the Eight Growth Factors

Use the eight growth factors to guide your listening and sharing. These growth factors have proven to be crucial to the process of helping others. Without them, no one can be helped.

1. Empathy (Active Listening). *Empathy* is different from *sympathy*. It has nothing to do with what *you* feel. Rather, it has to do with letting the other person know that you understand how *he or she* feels. Empathy is a form of communication. Empathy involves letting the person know that you have heard what he or she has said and that you know how the person feels about what he or she has said. This is done by repeating what you have heard. Through empathetic feedback you are saying, "I hear you; I know what you are saying." It does not matter how clearly you *understand* what is going on inside the other person. You cannot help the other person until you let the person know that you have heard him or her.

2. Warmth. Showing *warmth* is letting a person know that you care about him or her. The opposite of being warm is being cold, critical, judgmental, and distant. By showing warmth, you let the person know that he or she is important to you—that you genuinely like and appreciate him or her.

3. Respect. Respecting someone is simply accepting the person for whom he or she is. You respect a person's feelings and experiences. If a member of the group says, "I hate my mother," you do not say, "No, you don't." You accept what the person says, even if you disagree. You respect the person's feelings and experiences. You accept that what the person is saying is true—true to that person. You suspend all critical judgment of the person. This does not mean that you have to agree with his or her behavior or actions. You can accept a *person* and reject his or her *behavior*. Nor does this mean that you have to deny your own feelings and views. It simply means that you listen and allow the other person to be different.

4. Concreteness (Being Specific). Avoid being vague or general. One person can understand what another person is saying only if that person is specific. You can help someone to be specific by inviting the person to give examples or to be more exact in what he or she is saying.

5. Genuineness. Being genuine is being honest rather than being fake. It also is being spontaneous—not planned or rehearsed. All you have to do to be genuine is to be yourself—without trying to edit, censor, or shape how others see you. A genuine person does not cover up or hide things, nor does a genuine person make up things. A genuine person shares openly and honestly.

6. Self-Disclosure. Self-disclosure is talking about yourself and revealing yourself to others—your feelings, thoughts, and experiences. Avoid talking about others. If you must mention others, talk only about what directly affects you.

7. Confrontation. Confrontation is a form of honesty. It is important for others to know how we perceive them. Confrontation involves pointing out discrepancies that we see in others. There are three kinds of confrontation: 1) confrontation between opposing things that a person says, 2) confrontation between what a person says and what he or she does, and 3) confrontation between the self-awareness of the person sharing and the awareness of the listener.

8. Immediacy. Immediacy involves sharing what is going on right now in the group. The key is to focus on how what you are sharing affects you in the present moment, whether what you are sharing is a present struggle, a painful past experience, or a fear about the future.

Avoid Talking About Members Who Are Not Present

If we have a problem with a group member who is not present, we need to wait until that member is present before we talk about the problem. Finding out that the group talked about you while you were not present can be very painful. Also, if we want to deal with a problem that involves another member of the group, we need to get that person's permission before dealing with the problem in the group. If that person does not agree to discuss the problem, then the problem cannot be shared in the group.

All That Is Shared Is Confidential

Whatever is said in the group stays in the room. We are free to share anything that *we* have said in the group, but what someone else shares is not ours to share with another. If this guideline is violated, the group will die. No one will share anything important if he or she believes that it will be shared with others. Any report of a break in confidentiality will be investigated. Anyone who breaks confidentiality must face the group and deal with the members' feelings.

Do Not Use Names When Talking About Something That Involves Other People

Talking about other people is gossiping. The purpose of a sharing group is to talk about ourselves—our experiences, our lives, and our feelings. If we are relating an event that happened to us, then the group does not need to know the names of the other people involved. Names shift our focus from the person sharing to the story. When we are listening to someone share an experience that involves another person, we should not ask whom the person is or try to guess his or her identity. Our focus should be on the person who is sharing.

Do Not Attack One Another or People Outside the Group

Confrontation is a growth factor, and there are ways for confrontation to be used in the group. It is all right to be angry and to express that anger in appropriate ways, but it is not all right to attack one another or to call one another names. Attacks begin with second or third person pronouns, such as you, he, she, and they. To ensure that what we say is not an attack, we should use first person—I feel, I want, I wish, and so forth. As long as we are making I statements and are speaking about ourselves rather than others, we are speaking in a way that is helpful. Whenever we stop talking about ourselves—our feelings and experiences—and begin to talk about other people, we are tempted to attack or to get into the story.

Trust Yourself and Your Group

Trust your feelings and perceptions. Share when you feel it is appropriate, and trust the group. Over time, a group that follows these guidelines can and will help you.

Selected
Bibliography

The Sharing Group Format

Clinebell, Howard. *Growth Groups*. Nashville: Abingdon, 1977. This is an early work by a noted pastoral psychologist that applies the basics of group dynamics to non-clinical settings. One chapter is devoted to working with youth.

Clinebell, Howard. *The Mental Health Ministry Of The Local Church*. Nashville: Abingdon, 1972. Clinebell updates the information found in *Growth Groups* and specifically applies them to the local church setting.

Counseling Skills

Carkhuff, Robert. *Helping And Human Relations: Vol. 1*. Fort Worth: Holt, Rinehart & Winston, 1969. This book contains the basic research on which the sharing group model is based, including the eight growth factors. The work is extremely academic and not very readable.

Charry, Dana. *Mental Health Skills For Clergy*. Valley Forge: Judson, 1981. An excellent work that covers several key areas. It focuses on the referral process.

Clinebell, Howard. *Basic Types Of Pastoral Counseling*. Nashville: Abingdon, 1966. This basic counseling textbook which is used at many seminaries gives an overview of the fundamentals of counseling.

Olson, Keith. *Counseling Teenagers*. Loveland, CO: Group Books, 1984. This book which is written from a Christian perspective presents a conceptual framework as well as many techniques to use with teenagers.

Polster, Irving, and Miriam Polster. *Gestalt Therapy Integrated*. Santa Rosa: Vintage, 1973. This work presents a variety of counseling and therapy techniques developed by Gestalt therapists.

Savary, Louis M. et al. *Dreams And Spiritual Growth*. Mahwah, NJ: Paulist Press, 1984. This work offers a variety of techniques to use in the interpretation of dreams. It centers on using dreams as a means of spiritual growth.

Stone, David. *Friend To Friend: How to Help a Friend Through a Problem*. Loveland, CO: Group Books, 1983. This book presents a decision-making model that can be used in the counseling format. This model is helpful when someone needs to make a decision but is unable to do so.